LEFT TURN
AT
REALITY
CENTRAL

FURTHER ZEN RAMBLINGS
FROM THE INTERNET

SCOTT SHAW

BUDDHA ROSE PUBLICATIONS

10 9 8 7 6 5 4 3 2 1
Printed in the United States of America

LEFT TURN
AT REALITY CENTRAL

4

Introduction

Here it is, *The Scott Shaw Zen Blog 19.0,* originally presented on the *World Wide Web.* All of the writings presented in this book were written between December 2020 and April of 2021.

As was the case with the previously published volumes based upon *The Scott Shaw Zen Blog;* entitled: *Scribbles on the Restroom Wall, The Chronicles: Zen Ramblings from the Internet, Words in the Wind, Zen Mind Life Thoughts, The Zen of Life, Lies and Aberrant Reality, Apostrophe Zen, The Abstract Arsenal of Zen and the Psychology of Being, Zen and Again: The Metaphysical Philosophy of Psychology, Tempest in a Teapot and the Den of Zen, Buddha in the Looking Glass, Wo Ton' of the Blue Vision, Zen and the Psychology of the Spiritual Something, Pyrophoric Zen, Fragments of Paradox, Zen: Traversing the Entity of Non-Entity, Zen and the Ambient Echo: The Psychological Philosophy of Being, Paritical Zen and the Life Science of Becoming No Thing, Obscurist Occulto: Hiding from the Definition of Meaning, and Principles of the Precepts* this volume is presented exactly as it was viewed on *scottshaw.com* with no rewriting, punctuation, or typo corrections. From this, we hope you will receive the original reading experience.

This volume of internet ramblings is presented with the date and time listed as to when each blog was originally posted. Also, the blogs in this volume are presented from last to first. With this, we hope to present a transcendence back through time as opposed to an evolving evolution. In addition, we left out the traditional *Table of*

Contents in an attempt to leave this volume with a much more free-flowing reading experience.

Okay, there's the information and the definitions. Read on… We hope you enjoy it. And, be sure to stayed tuned for the ongoing *Scott Shaw Zen Blog @ scottshaw.com.*

You're Only Happy
When You Get What You Want
15/Apr/2021 01:01 PM

I believe for all of us there are those times when we walk into a store and find that perfect piece of clothing, that perfect piece of jewelry (for the ladies) or that perfect whatever, for a great price, and we walk out really happy. We got what we wanted. Maybe what got something that we didn't even know that we wanted but all of the planets aligned and all was well with the world. We got what we wanted and we are really happy about it.

But, is happiness only based upon getting what you want? Yes, for many it is.

If you ever take the time to watch people and their interactions with their happiness, or lack thereof, it is really obvious that for some they must get what they want to be happy. Things must be the way they want those things to be or they are unhappy. I currently know some people, and I have known people in the past, that the moment they do not get what they want they throw a major tantrum.

Why do some people do this? Why do some people base all of their okay-ness defined by whether or not they are getting what they want? I suppose there are a million psychologically based reasons for this. Mostly, however, I assume it is mainly based in the fact that as a child they subconsciously learned that if they screamed loud enough and for long enough that would equal them getting whatever it is that they desired.

I think if we look around, we see this all the time. And, this is not a mindset based solely on an individual getting that material something that they want. If a person is not behaving the way the other person wants them to behave, they throw a fit. If a person is not agreeing with what they thinks or believe, they throw a fit. If someone is not giving that desire-filled someone exactly whatever it is they desire, at the moment they want it, they throw a fit.

Once upon a time, in the not that long ago, pretty much all life interactions were based on the person-to-person concept. With the dawning of the age of the internet, all of this changed. Now, there are millions/billions of people interact that have no true idea of who that other person at the end of that screen name truly is. It is all an abstract nothing. Yet, there they are, two people (or more) demanding to be fulfilled, in whatever manner they define as fulfillment, by someone they may never meet face-to-face. Arguments break out, lies are told, deceptions are unleashed, and hurt is instigated, all for what? For one person to find a way to get what they want in order to experience that feeling of happiness.

How about you? Where do you find your happiness? When are you happy? What makes you happy? And, can you be happy when your desires are not being fulfilled and your wants and/or needs not met?

Few people really think about any of this. They just know the experience of happiness when they are getting what they want. But, can you (personally) make yourself happy when you are not getting what you want?

Here's the experiment for the day… Right now, whatever it is you are doing, whatever it is you are feeling, allow happiness to enter you. Allow yourself to become happy.

Even if you are sad. Even if you are pissed off at somebody or something. Even if you are felling that you are not getting what you want, let the happiness in.

If you practice this experiment, you can get really good at it. You will find that even when you are not happy you can create the space of happiness in your mind. And, from this, your entire world will get better because when you need that feeling of happiness, to change your frame of mind, you can invoke it.

The emotions you experience in your life are truly defined by you. They are truly defined by what you choose to feel. You can be unhappy when you don't get what you want. You can be happy when you do get what you want. Or, you can choose to raise your consciousness above all of that external stimuli stuff and enter a state of mind where you are in control of your emotions. From this, you will no longer be dominated by negative emotions. From this, you will no longer be driven down the path of doing bad things based upon your negative emotions of not getting what you want. From this, you can choose to be happy when you choose to be happy. And, because of this, you will make everyone who encounters you happy to be in your presence.

      *   *   *

14/Apr/2021 07:35 AM

Who do you like and why do you like them?

Who do you hate and why do you hate them?

If you have not clearly defined your feeling you can never truly understand why you feel your feelings.

Few people ever understand why an artist does what they do. Sure, there are a plethora of critics out there who wish to love or hate a piece of art and cast their opinion(s) onto it but they never truly understand why that artist created the piece of art that they did. Except for the artist themselves, few ever possess the ability to peer in the, *"Why,"* an artist.

Recently, Amazon has informed its millions of indie film production companies that they will be shifting away from the physical distribution of films via DVD. They wish to only focus on their On-Demand Streaming service. I get it, times are changing. Most everybody wants everything up there in the great abyss of the ethereal. Though it is sad to see it go, there is nothing that we, the indie filmmakers, can do. Like I always say, you can only play in your own playground. …Though there are many Zen Films up on the Amazon On-Demand platform, some are a bit too racy for their standards.

There are other services that offer DVD distribution. As such, I (we) have begun to move the entire Zen Film catalogue over to another distributor for those of you who still wish an actual physical copy of a movie. And, there are many of you. Due to this forced process, I have been given the opportunity to take a look at some of my previous films and clean up some of the audio and stuff like that. Many of these films I have not watched in many-many years.

One of these Zen Films is *Super Hero Central.* This is a fairly obscure Zen Film. When it was first released, on VHS, there seemed to be a lot of viewers. But, as time when on, that faded away. In fact, that is one of my few films that has not been hit with a lot of harsh reviews. ...Just giving you Reviewers out there the heads-up if you want to assault something that hasn't already been highly attacked.

Having the opportunity to look at it again, as the filmmaker, I can see—I can tell you about some of my mindset in its creation. ...For those few of you who actually care.

During the filming of this movie, my *Zen Filmmaking* brother, Donald G. Jackson was in his last days. He was very sick. Though I give DGJ Co-Producer credit, I filmed the nuts and bolts of the film solely as a Scott Shaw Zen Film, which is really very different from a Scott Shaw, Donald G. Jackson Zen Film. When it was done, I put the first cut together.

The thing was, just before my filming of this movie, and just before Don had gotten very sick, I had shot a large amount of footage about this Old-Hollywood character, played by Don. Due to the storyline of *Super Hero Central* it just hit, the two filmmaking excursions fit together perfectly. Thus, I went back into the film and combined the two. This became the first released version of the film but not the only. Like many of my Zen Films there is more than one version out in the out there.

Soon after this, however, DGJ left this place we call, *"Life."* You know, though we certainly had our ups and down, Don was genuine friend and a true partner in the crazed world of abstract/artistic filmmaking.

After his passing, something just struck me. At this point what I did was to go back into the film and do a re-cut. What I did, as a sort of a tribute, was to add a lot of footage from some of the previous Scott Shaw and Donald G. Jackson Zen Films as somewhat of homage to Don and to our filmmaking partnership. That is the longer version of the film and the one that is being re-released.

By this point in my career, 2003, I had begun to focus more and more on the more Zen, non-narrative elements of filmmaking. My emphasis was really shifting away from any story-driven narrative. In fact, SHC was probably one of my last films that truly took that route of storytelling.

So, for all you film critics out there, you now have some food for thought if you wish to write a critique. For all of you lovers/understanders of *Zen Filmmaking,* you now have a bit more insight into one of the least watched Zen Film, *Super Hero Central.*

Mostly, for all you artists out there, KEEP CREATING! Even if no one ever knows or understands why you do what you do—even if you find a ton of critics, be whole in knowing you are the one that is creating and isn't that one of best/greatest things anyone can do?

13/Apr/2021 07:15 AM

How much of what you believe is based upon what someone else has told you?

How much of what you do is based upon what someone else has suggested that you do?

How much of your life is actually your creation and how much of your life is a life defined by what other people have guided you to do?

The Voice of the People, The Changing of the Times, and Everybody is Fighting for What They Believe In
11/Apr/2021 05:13 PM

Certainly, at least in the United States, this has been a time of the attempt for rapid change. People have taken to the streets, protests have erupted, and destruction has ensued. The fact is, there is nothing new in all of this. Every now and then a subset of a culture stands up and cries out for change.

Several years ago, what became known as the *Arab Spring* was born. In the West, it was hoped and believed that this would lead to a new, more free and more democratic Middle East, where the peoples, the various religions, and the women would find more freedom. This, unfortunately, did not come to be the case.

Over the past recent months, in Myanmar, there has been upheaval about the military having taken control over the country once again. For those of us who have charted the political evolution of Myanmar we have watched a marginal loosening of military control occur over the past decade or so only to be reinstated. In fact, I was in then Burma, when a military coup took over the country, in the mid 1980's. The coup did things like completely wipe out the currency. The masses were upset. But, what could they do? Little has changed since then.

I have witnessed in seemingly open societies like Malaysia, where people of Chinese heritage, are treated very badly solely due to their race and their religion or lack thereof. ...Few people of

15

Chinese heritage in Malaysia practice the Islamic religion, which is the standard of that country.

The point being is that eventually, in all cultures, people find a motivation and they seek change. They desire to live a better more fruitful, less restricted life. This is most commonly the primary motivation leading to revolution. To achieve this, sometimes there is an uprising. But, what do these uprising actually equal?

Here in the U.S., the last time of large ongoing uprising occurred in the 1960s. Then, people were seeking a new freedom. They were rebelling against political and police control and the draft that was taking young American men to possibly die in Vietnam before they could even vote. For those of you who may not know, the draft took men as young as eighteen. But, it was not until 1971 that a U.S. citizen could vote before they reached the age of twenty-one. Thus, young men were dying but they could not even vote for the politicians who were sending them to the battlefield. Combine this with the ethnic and the police repression that was taking place and it gave birth to a movement of freedom seekers.

Times were changing and the strict morality of the previous generations was giving way to new freedoms: socially, emotionally, and sexually. People were seeking to live a life less defined by the moral restrictions of times gone past.

From this, a new mindset of freedom of movement and expression was given birth to. In fact, many of the people who have fallen under criticism in the world of today were simply basing their life, their lifestyle, and their life actions upon a mindset that was formulated and became accepted in that era. But, times change and we have entered into a much more restricted time period where people find their power by critiquing, criticizing, attacking, and even claiming illegality by people who are only exhibiting a lifestyle that was once quite accepted. ...An open and unrestricted lifestyle that people once fought to achieve is now seen as something bad.

Though some of the same motivating factors are still in place here in the U.S. today, what is obvious is that the 1960s protests where motivated by a new and freer mindset leading to a less restrictive lifestyle. Today, motivated by things like #metoo, #blm #woke, #cancelculture people are seeking to, *"Blame," "Rebuke,"* and, *"Cancel,"* a person that they find to have spoken something, did something, or lived a life of too much unrestricted freedom. Seemingly gone is even a person's ability to speak their mind without being chastised and in some cases fired for doing so. Meaning, they, (the undefined masses), wish to hold a particular person responsible simply for saying or doing something that the person believe they possessed the right to do.

Certainly, hurting anyone is wrong under any circumstance. But, who is actually hurting whom and why? And, where does the blame actually lie?

What is occurring now is that people are blaming others instead of looking to themselves and making a true and clear assessment of what they, personally, have done to others and to our society as a whole by the actions they have untaken and the lifestyle they have lived. It is so much easier to join the masses in a protest, blaming whomever for whatever, than it is to look deeply into one's self and take on the responsibility for the thing(s) that they, (that you), have done wrong. My question/statement to anyone accusing others has always remained the same, *"What have you done wrong? Who have you hurt? What have you done to fix any damage you have created?"*

I think back to my youth, and I am sure I have mentioned this in this blog in the past, but there were times when my friends and I would go into a restaurant and we would not be served simply because we dressed the style of the day and we had long hair. And, that was in Hollywood, California. Think what was going on in the rest of the country. To us, we were the vehicles. We were rebelling and hoping to shape a new expression of culture. But, to the workers at those establishment we were, *"Hippies,"* or whatever other noun they wished to refer to us as. They considered us wrong for being who we were? Where we wrong for being a part of the change? Were they wrong for holding onto the past and believe what they believed? The fact is, that is all a point of view. No one is right. No one is wrong. It is simply your individual perception.

So, as you pass through your life you really need to keep this in mind—particularly at a period like this where there is a large attempt at change. Think about what you are attempting to change and why are you trying to change it? Think about whom in your past has tried to change you and why did they believe you needed to change? Think about whom you have hurt by what you have done or are doing and question what are you doing to make yourself right and correct any wrongs you have done?

Who is ultimately right? Who is ultimately wrong? It is easy to cast your judgment. It is easy to take to the party in the streets, which is disguised as a protest. But, what are you actually doing to make your society any better? Better always begins with you cleaning up yourself and cleaning up any mess you have made in the life of another individual. Change truly begins with one-on-one. As I always say, *"I'm sorry,"* is one of the best mantra anyone can embrace.

You can try to make an external change. But, if all you are doing is attacking someone else for them being who they are, you have missed the entire point of human evolution.

You Don't Get an Award for
How Much You Meditate
10/Apr/2021 09:57 AM

As the martial arts were born in Asia there is commonly a very strong connection between the martial arts and the various schools of Taoism and Buddhism; all of which place a very heavy focus upon meditation. Though meditation may be marginally embraced in some schools of the martial arts, most schools commonly center all of their attention upon self-defense, fight training, and moving up the belt ladder until the practitioner ultimately earns a black belt. But, you do not earn a black belt for how long or how well you meditate.

If you look at the martial arts, if you look to its practitioners, if you look to the people who watch and/or admire the martial arts via movies, books, magazine, and other outlets, what you commonly see and hear are people discussing how good or bad they believe a practitioner to be—they discus who can beat up who and who would win in a real world fight. Listen to an advanced martial arts practitioner and they will almost universally mention the fact that they have earned a black belt. But, you do not earn a black belt for how long or how well you meditate.

As a practitioner of the martial arts for most of my life, when I was a student, I trained under several very well respected and rank-advanced instructors. All of whom were Asian born. In each case, at the end of each class, they would either have the students sit or stand for a moment of meditation. *"Mun yum,"* as it is stated in the Korean language. We would close our eyes for a moment but then the handclap would come and that would be that. Class over. There was no real time made for true meditation.

When we would test for rank advancement, some schools and some organizations would dictate a moment of meditation before the trial. It was proclaimed to be a moment to focus your body and your mind before the grueling test. But, it was only for a moment. At best, it was only a situation created where our anxiety level would rise based upon questioning our own competence. It was not true meditation.

In my own life, though I was formally involved with the martial arts since I was six years old, meditation and its practice was something that I pursued very separate from what would appear to be two coalescing trainings. My study and my practice of meditation was something that I viewed as a completely separate pathway. Even when I began teaching the martial arts on a professional level, when I was in college, I understood that meditation is not why most people joined my school. Sure, meditation sounds good. Sure, meditation has all of those promised benefits. But, does a student wish to take time out of a one-hour class to sit on the floor of the dojang and meditate? For most, the answer was, *"No."*

In movies and on TV shows you always see the martial art star meditating. But, is that real life? Is that what they actually do? For the most part, the answer to that question is, *"No."* And, I personally know a few of these people. And, they do not make meditation an actual part of their life. When they are interviewed, they may claim that they do. But, claiming that you do does not equal actual meditation.

Why do so few people meditate? Why do so few martial artists meditate? The answer is because there is very little obvious reward. You cannot tell people, *"I meditated for an hour today,"* and expect to earn a black belt and a diploma you can place on your wall because of that feat.

All of this leads us to the fact of why meditation is such a unique element of life. It is unique because you have to choose to do it. You will not earn an award for doing it. You will not be able to beat someone up because you do it. You will not get big muscles because you do it. You will not get a diploma to hang on your wall because you, *"Sit,"* for ten minutes, fifteen minutes, or an hour a day. The only reward is something that is so internal that it cannot even be rightly put into words.

So, as in all cases, your life is your choice. What you do with it is what you do with it. What are you going to do with your life? Are you only going to do all of that Outside Stuff, where you can find reward, gratitude, and diplomas to hang on your wall, or are you going to find a pathway to an indescribable passageway to mental awareness? Your life, your choice.

*　　*　　*

10/Apr/2021 09:14 AM

As long as you are focusing your concentration on someone else that means that you are not focusing on improving yourself.

*   *   *

10/Apr/2021 07:33 AM

Once that time has been wasted it can never be
wasted again.

24

*　　*　　*
10/Apr/2021 07:32 AM

If you don't ask for help you won't receive any help.

*   *   *

09/Apr/2021 02:45 PM

You can only work with what there is to work with.

*   *   *

09/Apr/2021 02:19 PM

When you're tired of doing it's time to start undoing.

*   *   *

08/Apr/2021 07:29 PM

The people who ask for the most generally give the least.

08/Apr/2021 07:29 PM

Do you think more about what you have done or do you think more about what you haven't done?

The Way People Expect Their Zen
08/Apr/2021 09:10 AM

Let's face it, people are all the same. No matter how nonconformist, revolutionary, in-the-know, or cool a person considers themselves to be they too are pretty much just the same as the very-traditional person who lives next door.

Some people are drawn to the more abstract realms of human reality. Some people seek out the knowledge promised to be known by other cultures and/or the, *"Knowers."* Some people believe that they are seeking and perhaps are existing in that realm of, *"Different,"* inhabited by the very few. But again, let's face the facts, except for the clothing a person wears, how they style their hair, the tattoos they place on their skin, or what they speak based upon what they believe they know, nothing about them is very different from the anybody else.

You can choose to live in a monastery but how does that make you any better than the person who raises a family and goes to work everyday struggling to pay the bills to give their children a better life than he or she had? You can live on the streets; living rent free and taking food, clothing, and whatever other help anyone will throw your direction but how does that differ from the person who lives at their parent's house and does not leave the nest of comfort?

People who seek knowledge expect it come at them in a manner that they understand. They want it to be presented in words that their mind comprehends and accepts. People want the promise of life everlasting and reward for their life strife. This is why the churches and the preachers, in whatever domination, in whatever country on earth, are the most successful when they give the people exactly what they want. They promise them the desired promise in a language that they can easily understand.

For example, who makes the most money off of claiming to interpret and then pass on the understanding of an abstract concept of reality such as Zen? Answer: The people that present it in the most comprehensible and conventional fashion. But, is that true Zen or is that simply a minimalized presentation of Zen designed to make it understandable by the people who could never truly understand it? But, an essential factor that must be kept in mind in all of this is that, without the common folk filling the temples the temples would not exist?

A religion or a philosophy only thrives when it is present in a manner that can be comprehended by those who need things to be simple. This is the common state of humanity. People need things to be simple. They wish to be presented with a truth that they can easily understand and do not need to think too hard about for it to become something that they can believe in.

Think about it… What do you believe and why do you believe it? How hard was it for you to comprehend, analyze, and internalize what you believe? How much time do you/did you spend delving deeply into the essence of what you believe before you came to the conclusion that you believed it?

True knowledge is something that is very complex. True knowledge is something that goes far beyond belief. But, how few are the people that possess the mental aptitude to be able to remove all of the promised illusion and simplicity of any belief system and truly go to the source of their own foundations for belief?

You can believe what you're told if you want to. You can listen to anyone who is speaking and believe whatever it is they have to say if that is your mental makeup. But, this will never allow you to find the true essence of reality on any level.

If all you do is believe, then all you do is believe. Remember, just because you think you believe something that does not necessarily make it the truth.

So, I am sitting here in the late night, as I tend to do. Some people are very upset about their sleeplessness when they do not sleep. Though I love sleep, (one of my favorite things to do), but it never bothers me when I do not sleep, as there is only so much life we are given to live.

I've doused my body and mind with the grape, as I tend to do. I've watched a movie or two—On-Demand; barely worth watching, as is the promised. I have a Persian cat sitting on my lap, awake like I, purring loudly, as we are both very happy to be in one another's company. All that's a good thing…

Generally, before I go to bed, in these days of late, I tend to watch music videos late into the late night. Most, I've seen before. Some are new. Some, from the first generation of music videos, bring back memories. But, all of them cast me to a space of altered reality where my mind may melt with the abstract realms of rhythm, melody, and visual images.

Sometimes, I flip over to CMT and watch County Music Videos for a time. It always makes me think, *"You really should have made me a Country Western Superstar."* I mean, I have written so many songs that would play so well as Country… I could have so expanded in that world of blonde and fake blonde people. But, that was never who I truly was. I guess I was way too dark for all of that… But, I could have been/should have been… If you know what I mean…

Mostly, I watch and listen to what is new. I love the feel-good because so much of life is just the opposite. I love the grand vision of the subtleties. Most of the video, like the music, is expected: heard and seen before. I don't know if the directors of these pieces ever truly consciously know what they are creating but every now and then they hit a note of excellent in their cinematic presentations. Then, at least for a moment, life is filled with perfection.

It's funny... One those things that most people of the world do not know... ...Something that my lady and I just spoke about this evening as we watched this Academy Award nominated actor now doing a, *"Cheap,"* film On-Demand late into the late night... ...Stars are everywhere here in L.A. You see them all the time. As I was born here, it just seemed like that was the way it is. I never thought that much about it. Because what does fame really mean anyway?

Anyway, this one guy, (the aforementioned actor), we were eating this great pasta-based breakfast at this restaurant in We-Ho a while back, pre-pandemic, outside as I like to sit and he was there smoking—really killing our meal standing just outside of the railing talking to this actress who currently had a popular TV series. Academy Award nomination or not, this one-time star had the potential to kill the experience of the everyday person just like everyone else has the potential to do. But, who thinks about anyone else, especially when you were once nominated for an Academy Award? Do you? How much time do you spending thinking about how what you are doing may affect the someone/the anyone else?

I think to when I am on an A-movie set. Pretty much they have Still Photographers and Videographers capturing all that they can. Every now and then I notice that one of these people knows who I am. ...They know the who they think I am. I can see them wondering, *"What is this guy doing here?"* But, they photograph me none-the-less. I wish I could have all of those photographs. I wish I could have all of those videotapes. They would make a great Zen Film.

That is not to say that all are aghast that Scott Shaw would be cast in something big. Some know me. Some are very nice to me—happy that I am there. Me too But, it is more the notice of those who expect the obvious that wonder why the dis-obvious would ever be cast in such a role that makes me smile.

But, this leads us to the all and the everything of the nothing... The essence of life, for those of us who care to see it. And, the Lost Vision of Suchness... If we look to the abstract we can see the subtle actuality of the conceptual vision of reality. If we can see the ego of those who are verses the minds of those who are not we can find that center point and come to the understanding that no matter where a person finds themselves in life it is what they do with that placement that makes them less or more—that makes them controlled by or a participant to the understanding of the great illusion.

You can know, if you want to know. You can be, if you want to be. Or, you can simply exist, controlled by all the, *"Out there."*

Who are you? What are you? What are you trying to become?

Can you be what you can be? Or, must you only be what is seen and defined in the eyes of the everyone else?

35

*   *   *

06/Apr/2021 01:08 PM

What would your life be like if you got to live every fantasy you ever had?

*   *   *

06/Apr/2021 08:59 AM

Everybody sees the obvious. Few people seek out the subtleties.

*   *   *

04/Apr/2021 08:27 AM

Nobody wants to be reminded of their mistakes.

*   *   *

03/Apr/2021 07:08 AM

There are specific levels of Higher Consciousness that an individual can achieve but if a person does not walk on the Path of Higher Consciousness they can never experience or embrace this transformation.

*   *   *

02/Apr/2021 09:04 AM

If you don't get your hands dirty, you're not going to get your hands dirty.

01/Apr/2021 09:40 AM

You can live in denial all you want but denial never changes what you have done.

Most people operate from a perspective and the knowledge that they will be here tomorrow—that what they do today is going to set the stage for what is going to happen tomorrow. For some, however, they know that tomorrow will not be here so they do not care about what they unleash, because whatever they unleash is not going to affect them in any great manner.

This occurrence may be predicated by numerous factors. Certainly, a person's age and health is a big one. If a person is old and/or dying they know their time is short so, in many cases, they just don't care what they say or do because fuck everybody, they are on their way out. This is also the case with people who are young. As we all understand, the young believe that there will always be a tomorrow. So, whatever they do today, no matter how heinous it may be, everything will be new tomorrow—there will be new chances and new opportunities.

A good example of the age factor is, here in the U.S., we have a newly elected president. The guy is old. There is no other way to describe him but old. I mean, he is seventy-eight years old making him the oldest person ever elected to the presidency of the United States of America. He has come into office and is throwing all his power around like many a new president has done in the past. But, what he is doing is really creating a lot of short-term and long-term damage to the country. Though he is promising, maybe even believing, that what he is doing is right, people are already suffering. But, let's look at the facts; he is old. He's not going to be around to view the long-term affects of his declarations. What does he care?

From a personal perspective, which also goes to the case-in-point of this discussion, I think back to when one of books was about to be published by a division of *Simon and Schuster. The Warrior is Silent: Martial Arts and the Spiritual Path* was set to be released and they sent me the almost-final proofed copy of the book for me to do one final read and then approve or disapprove of what the editors had done. The thing was, some stupid editor had gotten into the manuscript and did this weird, (very New Age), thing of instead of referring to the colloquial, *"He or Him,"* as is common to the English language, throughout the book they periodically exchanged, *"He and Him,"* with *"Her and She."* It just made the read of the manuscript bad! I contacted the Senior Editor and told, *"Him,"* I hated it. He said he would have it changed back to the way I had presented the manuscript and would have the editor of the book contact me. *"She,"* did.

The moment she got on the phone I could tell she was in a pissy mood. I asked about it and she told me she had just been let go (fired) and that this was her last day on the job and the redoing of this book was her last gig for the company. This worried me but she said she would do the job at hand. What could I do but let her promise play out? Maybe a month or so later, I got the author release of the book, she had done nothing! He and She were left interchangeable. But, what did she care? She had already been fired. She didn't give a shit. And, for me, (the author), the book had already been set to print, so there was nothing that I could do.

43

This is the thing; there are some people who just have nothing left to lose. So, they don't care what they do or whom they do it to.

On the street, you will sometimes see a criminal with that, *"Nothing left to lose,"* look in their eyes. I always warn people they are the worst people to go up against in a street fight because not only are they ruthless, as they have nothing to lose, they are almost impossible to defeat.

So... Most of us don't find ourselves embracing this state of mind. ...At least not yet... We care about our tomorrow and we care about how what we do today will affect someone else's tomorrow. But, the fact of the matter is, there will come a time in each of our lives when we will fall under the domination of someone who just doesn't give a fuck about us. Then what???

The Answer: Really, I don't know. The thing about life is that you can't control what you can't control. There's really not much you can do. The only thing you can do—the only thing you do have control over is you. You, and how you react.

So, just be prepared... Sooner or later you are going to get screwed over by someone who does not care about how what they are doing is going to do to you.

Maybe you can kick their ass, maybe you can yell and scream at them. But, most likely, there will be nothing you can do. So, you are just going to have live with their uncaring doing. Not right, but welcome to life.

Who is it that you would like to reconnect with?

What person that is no longer in your life would you like to touch base with once again?

Maybe the relationship ended because they hurt you. Maybe the relationship ended because you hurt them. Maybe you moved away from one another. Or, maybe you simply let your communication channels fade.

Some people want to thank someone from their past. Some people want to say, *"I'm sorry."* Some people miss the conversations, the mental stimulation, the creativity, or just the fun they had with that someone out there.

Some people want to get back in touch with someone because they feel that is the person, *"Who got away."* Maybe one person loved the other person but, for whatever reason, the together-relationship did not work out at that time. Maybe two people worked well together but, for whatever reason, one of them moved on. Maybe two people simply begin following separate paths in life. Though there are an untold number of reasons why people come together and then move apart, that does not necessarily have to be the end-all to the story. This is the age of the internet, people are easy to find. If they are still alive, you could probably find a means to contact them if you tried.

Some people are very clear when they move away from someone who inhabited their past. They did it for a reason and they stick to that logic. In some cases, breaking away from an individual has occurred because some people do some pretty stupid or bad things. But, people can learn. People can evolve. People can change. Have you changed? Maybe you have. Maybe you want to let that someone know that you have. How can they know unless you tell them? How can they redefine how they feel about you unless you let them know who and what you have become?

The thing to keep in mind in all of this is that this entire concept is a bit touchy of a subject. Some people have moved on with their life and particularly their relationships. Does a husband or a wife want an old flame to be contacting their partner? Probably not. You should respect that. But, there are so many other variant in all of this, so many reasons that one person may wish to reconnect with someone from their past, that as long as you (as long as anyone) is doing this with a pure spirit, good things may come from reconnecting if both people are willing. You won't know unless you try.

Speed Kills But Who Cares?
30/Mar/2021 04:12 PM

I live in this community that is situated up on top of a hill. As it is on a hill, anytime you leave, via the very few streets that take you away from this area, you are going to go down a hill. Sometimes people travel vey fast down these streets. In fact, just last month, Tiger Woods crashed his SUV driving down a street I transverse virtually everyday.

As I often say, even very recently in this blog, you can learn a lot about a person and about humanity in general by witnessing the way people drive.

In any case, I was leaving the hill today. I was en route to pick up a new battery for my motorcycle. As I was going down hill, via this one street—not the one Tiger crashed on but the road just one street over, this shinny new black SUV jams by.

This is a two-lane street that is quite steep. Steeper than the one Tiger crashed on. Two cars were going neck-and-neck, blocking anyone from passing. Though I hate it when people do this, I generally sit back until one car goes faster or slower and I can get by. This SUV, on the other hand, jammed past, to the right of the car in the slow lane. I kinda don't know how he did it, as this is not a wide street, but he made it.

My thought was, *"I'd never seen that before."*

As I drove father down the hill, I began to see a bunch of smoke, then I started to smell the scent of burning brakes. I looked around, and just up ahead, I saw the SUV at a dead stop in the slow lane. Stupidly, this lady up in front of me, comes to a complete stop right next to the SUV in the fast lane. I wasn't going that fast and could stop but I honked at her to get out of the way because, as mentioned, a lot of people drive down these hills very fast. She pulled out of the way.

I looked over at the SUV, the driver was apparently going too fast and couldn't make the turn. He had smashed into the cement dividing wall, eventually ending up over in the slow lane with the car all jacked up and all of the airbags deployed. All I saw were the airbags but no person.

Me, I drove on...

You know, life is a lot like this... Some people want to be somewhere and they want to be there fast. But, many don't make it and they crash along the way. Some people do what they do, as hastily as possible, and they don't care who they hurt in the process. In this case, as in Tiger's case, it was just the driver who got hurt. I'm assuming there was only one person in the SUV but I don't really know. The thing is, though other people didn't get hurt, at least not obviously, in these two cases, this is not always the case. Think how many people crash their cars into other people due to impatience or a need for speed. It has happened to me. Has it happened to you?

They say, patience is a virtue. I agree. I also agree that sometimes it isn't that simple. Sometimes you've got a place you need to be.

I remember, way back in the way back when, I had this girlfriend living in an apartment by Santa Monica beach and I had a place in Hollywood. She called me up one night all freaked out that there had been this purv peeking in through her window. I got on my bike (motorcycle), knowing it would be the fastest, and jammed the thirty miles. I was popping stop signs, stoplights, fully adrenalized hoping she would be okay and ready to kick some guys ass. Luckily, I made it there safely and she was okay. I took her back to my place with me. But then, me, I had the motivation to speed. It was the right thing that I believed I must do. As stated, luckily I made it okay, but what if I had not. Then what? And, this is the thing, we all have motivations for doing what we do; some are very altruistic. But, if we hurt others in our doing, if we hurt ourselves, then what? What will anything have meant?

So, when you do what you do, think about what you are doing. Because in all life events there are more people than just you who are involved. Sometimes even the people you don't know and will never know may become involved.

Always keep in mind; no life is alone and separately isolated solely onto itself. Whatever you do affects the someone else; even if that someone else is a person you will never meet.

Remember, speed kills.

*　　*　　*

29/Mar/2021 02:51 PM

How much will it cost you to get what you want?

*   *   *

29/Mar/2021 09:43 AM

When you woke up this morning was your first thought, *"Who am I going to help today?"* If it wasn't, what does that say about who and what you are?

*   *   *

27/Mar/2021 08:25 PM

You don't do anything right with the wrong intention.

You don't do anything wrong with the right intention.

"The cause of suffering is desire." This is one of the most perfectly profound statements ever made about the human condition. It was spoken by Siddhartha Gautama, the Sakyamuni Buddha.

Like Jesus Christ, little is factually known about The Buddha. His history and teachings were recorded by those who lived after his worldly presence, which is believed to have ended in approximately 483 BCE. Though he was not the one who recorded or wrote his teachings, the words that are attributed to him are quite profound.

Though much of the world is going back into a mode of lockdown due to a sharp rise in the cases of COVID-19, here is California, as vaccinations are being performed and cases are diminishing, some of the COVID-19 pandemic lockdown protocols are being lifted. Some establishments are being allowed to open on a limited basis. Among them are churches and temples.

There is this very expansive Buddhist temple situated here in Southern California. It is very reminiscent of those located in Asia. It has been closed to the public over the past year.

As things are opening up, I thought I would check to see if I would be able to revisit the temple. Yes, they are now open but due to the fact that things are opening slowly, and there are still restrictions as to how many people may enter an establishment, one must make an appointment to go there.

The interesting thing I found about all of this is that on their website they state that people may make an appointment to go there but they may only enter for a short period of time to pray. Now, at least to me, this is very interesting. And, it is something that truly provides a look into the mindset of humanity.

The entire premise of The Buddha's teaching is about emancipation. It is about spiritual liberation. It is about the loss of desire in order to meet Nirvana. The Buddha did not want followers, as say did Jesus. In fact, he did not accept them. *"Are you are god? No, I'm just a man. Are you are guru? No, I'm just a man."* Yet, throughout the evolution of Buddhism there have been those who have prayed to his idealized image. But, as in the case with Christianity, isn't that simply idol worship? Yes, of course, people claim that they are only praying to that construct as a focal point, but why pray to an image at all? And, moreover, if you are praying to The Buddha, aren't you missing the entire essence of true Buddhism?

What this tells us about people and humanity is that most need to believe in that something bigger than themselves. They need that god. They need to believe that someone/something Out There will be there to help them in their time of need. But, what is need? Isn't need simply something that you want? Thus, it is desire but desire goes against the entire core teaching of Buddhism.

Is you don't want anything... Is you want nothing to be different... Then, there is no need to pray. What would you be praying for?

It's important to remember, that even praying for the betterment of someone or something else is simply your desire for things to be different. If you hope for things/anything to be different than you are locked into a space of desire. Thus, you miss the entire a point of what The Buddha actually taught. *"The cause of suffering is desire."*

I think we all have been watching on the news how there has been a lot of standing up against the anti-Asian racism that has been going on recently; especially since the pandemic. Though this style of racism is nothing new, it seems to have been brought into focus due to the attacks on people of Asian descent that have been taking place of late. But, I guess some people just do not get the message.

As many of you know, I work a lot with vintage synthesizers in order to create music. I use a lot of the newer ones, as well, but it simply seems that the synths of times gone past provide a really unique sound. I release a lot of synth-based music and I hold back a lot more—for times to come. In any case, I'm always exploring new possibilities in sound.

I've recently decided to pick up this one synthesizer created a couple of decades back. I saw one in excellent condition, with the make an offer opinion, being offered on eBay so I contacted the person to find out just what they would take for it. In doing so, I mentioned I was looking to pick up a tested model in excellent condition either from here in the U.S. or Japan. The message I got back truly surprised me. The first line of it was, *"Never buy anything from those Jap bastards."* Wow! Someone certainly hasn't gotten the memo.

I just don't know how anyone, in this day and age, would not put a muzzle on language like that; especially to someone they did not even know. Maybe I'm a, *"Jap."*

You know, as I have spoken about over the years, there is a lot of ongoing racism in this world. Maybe it is the blacks focusing on the whites, the Asians focusing on the whites and the black, or the whites focusing on whomever. No matter who it is, it doesn't make it right. Speaking badly about anyone, simply due to his or her race, is just BAD. A person is a person is a person. Who they are is based upon who they are. Who they are is based upon what they do, and how they do it, to other people. They are not solely defined by their race.

You know, there is really very little we can do about this style of behavior. Saying something or criticizing a person who speaks like this is not going to change their mind. The one thing we can do is not be that person. Do not be the person who judges someone else. Do not be the person who criticizes someone else—especially based solely upon his or her race.

Good people do and say good things. I get it, so many people in this world gain their power by acts of negativity and hurtful actions. All I can say is, don't be that person. Be the person of positivity who hurts or attacks no one. Be the person who other people feel positively inspired by being around.

In terms of that synth, I guess I will have to buy it from someone else. Maybe someone in Japan.

Tick Tock:
Watching the Clock Tick Towards Your Death
25/Mar/2021 09:54 AM

For anyone who has ever had an animal in their life, you understand how they truly become a part of the family. I always find that the people who have never had a pet (I don't really like that term but you get my meaning) never truly understand companionship. You form a bond with that living creature. You love them and they love you. You take care of them and they give you all kinds of indescribable everything.

As most animals do not live as long as humans, it is truly devastation when they pass on. Some of my most emotional losses have come when one of my animal friends has left this life.

A few weeks back, we took one of our cats to the vet to have her yearly checkup. This cat is getting a bit older but she seems very healthy. The vet told us her kidneys were deteriorating and that there's a ninety-five percent chance that she will not live more than a year or two. Wow! That's a big one!

The thing is though, think about this, we know her life expectancy; she does not. We know when she is supposed to die. But, she does not. She is just living her life as best as she can. I believe she's happy. She has her routines; her likes and her dislikes. She is passing through her days but does not know her clock is ticking.

In life, we are all going to die. That's the reality. The reality that no one wants to think about. Most of us don't know when it will happen.

In my life, I have been right up against the wall of life and death a couple of times. The first time was when I was three. The next-door neighbor, to my grandmother, pushed me off of her porch, because I was white, and I got a compound fracture on my elbow. I'm told that I went into complete cardiac arrest one night while I was in the hospital. I don't remember that, though I do have those medical records. I do, of course, remember the hospital and that it was a pretty scary experience for a three year old, being without family at night and stuff like that. But, I lived.

I have experienced a few other very close calls. Of course, being hit on my motorcycle by a car when I was twenty-one, where my skull was fractured in numerous places; I was definitely knock, knock, knocking on heaven's door. But, there has been others times where I was very conscious and came face-to-face with the experience. Rock climbing as a teenager, I lost my grip and started uncontrollably sliding down the rock face. I closed my eyes. I mentally let go, knowing I was going to die. But, amazingly/magically my foot caught on a rock just at the edge of the gorge that kept me from going over the cliff. There was a time when I was a kid, just after my father died, and my uncle was driving me to his hometown and these Native-Americans ran us off of the road in Arizona. The car flipped, I saw what looked to be my passenger window breaking, I knew I was going to die. I let go… But, I didn't die. I OD'd on coke one night back in the 80s. Don't try that at home children… But anyway, I've been close a few times.

I think on a certain level, in some ways, the best way to go is quick and unexpected. My father instantaneously died of a massive heart attack. He was still in his forties. But, he went out quick.

59

I have also known people that knew death was oncoming. Most of them, I found, did nothing different. They didn't dig deep into their psyche and find any deeper meaning to their life or what was to come. A few, one in particular, who had been a total asshole to a lot of people, apologized to some of those people on his deathbed. Though a nice gesture, I don't know what good that really did. Did it change what he had done? No.

So, here's the thing, and this is something that we all need to think about; we are all going to die. Right now, most of us don't know when. And, that's a good thing. For some of us, it will come quickly, in a flash of light. For others, it will be a long slow process. But, the question you must keep in your mind is what are you doing right now to prepare for that moment when you are no more? What has your life meant? Who have you helped? Who have you hurt? And, what are you going to do right now, today, to make yourself a meaningful expression of existence if you leave this life tomorrow?

*   *   *

If a book could provide you with enlightenment why wouldn't everyone read it?

*   *   *

22/Mar/2021 06:58 AM

Think about all of the ants you have stepped on and
the spiders you have killed. Think about all of the
hamburgers, hotdogs, steaks, ham, fried chicken,
and bacon you have eaten. What would those
creatures lives have been like if you did not
orchestrate their demise?

All actions have consequences.

*　　*　　*

If you sandpaper any piece of wood long enough it becomes sawdust.

*   *   *

How many words do you speak that do not need to be spoken?

*   *   *

19/Mar/2021 09:15 AM

Who are you and why are you?

Recently, on the news, there has been a lot of stories about Asians being attacked by people of other races. The conclusion that many/most have reached is that this has been motivated due to the COVID-19 Coronavirus pandemic of 2020 continuing into 2021 that pretty much turned everyone's life upside down. But, is that true, is that the reality?

Throughout my life, I have heard a lot of talk about how one race of people considers themselves superior to another. I have long made the joke that if you want to see why the white race is superior all you have to do is watch the television series COPS. Of course, at least at this point in history, shows like COPS and Live PD have been removed from the airways due to all of the racial tension in air. And yes, watching those shows, for the most part, only illustrates people at the lowest rung of the ladder. But, in front of your eyes, you could see how many people, of all races, truly embrace the lowest level of human existence.

Personally, I find this condemnation of Asian races quite curious. For me, I grew up respecting and, in fact, putting some people of Asian decent on a pedestal. I mean, people of Asian descent trained me in the martial arts. This is the same with my schooling in the Eastern meditative disciplines. I, and many people of my clique, put an undo respect onto people of Asian origins simply because we believed they knew something that we did not.

As time in my life passed along, I certainly came to understand that simply because a person came from Asia that did not necessarily make them a good person. I have been cheated by a lot of people of Asian descent. This being said, I believe this critical focus going towards Asian has a much deeper root than simply COVID-19.

Sure, I'm pissed at China for allowing the creation of the virus and releasing that virus, whether knowingly or not, onto the world. I'm also pissed at them for what they did to Tibet, what they are doing to Hong Kong, and what they want to do to Taiwan. But, that is the Powers-That-Be that is not an individual person. The individual on the street cannot and should not be blamed for anything simply because of their race.

Interestingly, yesterday on the news, some young buck, thirty-something, white man attacked an elderly Asian-American woman in San Francisco. In the coverage, her face was bruised as he apparently went up to her and punched her in the face but he was the one being taken to the hospital as she was carrying a walking stick, fought back, and gave him a good beating. Good for her!

There has been many discussions, illustrations, news and cellphone footage depictions of Asians being attacked in the United States. But, who are they being attacked by and why? Whatever the race of the attacker, that person is simply looking for a reason to hate. And, this is one of the biggest problems in the world; some people look for a reason to hate and a person to take their own inner-disharmony out upon. If you are whole, complete, satisfied, and actualized within yourself, you never focus on the negative of anyone or anything. It is only those of small-mind, of unresolved identity issues, or a lack of true personal understanding that lashes out on anyone. They do this because it is easier for them to hurt someone else than to look within, finding their own flaws, and forging at path of expanding human and personal understanding that will actually make them a better, more compete, more whole and giving individual.

Look at the people who attack anyone in anyway, no matter what their race is, what is their motivation? It is to hurt someone outside of themselves. It is to judge someone simply for being whom and what they are. Who has that right? No one. Yet, this type of mindset flourishes all across all societies and it has been going on forever. Is it right? No. But, does, *"What is right,"* stop the attacker? No, it does not. Why? Because they are too locked within their own dissatisfaction with their own life. They want to blame someone else for their own lack of fulfillment. But, they are too unenlightened to be aware of this fact, so they lash out at whatever victim they can find. And, as can be seen, they generally go after the person that is older, weaker, or has no way to respond. Meaning, people that do this kind of stuff are cowards. And few get the beat down with the cane of an old woman as I previously discussed.

What can we learn from this? What can you learn from this? Answer: If you are focusing your judgment, your condemnation, or your anger outside of yourself all you are doing is illustrating to the world your limited perception of the rightness of human reality.

Each person is good and whole onto themselves. Yes, some people do bad things but that bad thing is not categorically defined by their race. In fact, just the opposite. Good people do good things. Bad people do bad things. Does a white or black person become better by coming up behind an elderly Asian individual and shoving them down and into the street as has been illustrated in news footage? No. That is a coward.

If you don't like someone, ask yourself why? If you don't like an entire race, simply because of their race, you really need to take a look at your inner foundational elements. All goodness, all rightness comes from a positive place within. Develop that within yourself. Never judge or hurt anyone. Be more than the people who are less. Don't judge. Don't hurt. Make this world a better place.

Is That Anyway to Live
AKA Controlled By Your Demons
17/Mar/2021 09:40 AM

Yesterday, in the greater L.A. area, a house blew up. Apparently, they had a large amount of illegal professional grade fireworks stored on the property. The news showed all of the door cam and iPhone footage from nearby residences and they had a helicopter overhead. It was a massive show of fireworks exploding in the air.

The explosion killed two people (so far) and destroyed a lot of nearby residences. But, why did this happen? It happened because a person or persons was only thinking about themselves and not about the anyone or the anything else. Is that anyway to live?

In the overheard helicopter footage it showed a fireman leading a horse away from the debris. Luckily, the horse seems very tame and responsive to the fireman's help. But, think about that poor horse. We, as humans, we can process and figure out what took place. But, a horse has no basis of information or knowledge. To him (or her) it was simply Armageddon.

I have always been a strong opponent against keeping horse locked up in cages AKA stalls. I mean, how is that anyway for a horse to live their life. They should be running free in a field.

A few years back I wrote about how in my neighborhood there are a lot of people who keep horses as pets. Some even ride them down a busy thoroughfare. That is just not right! Caged is not where a horse should be. How would you like to be locked up in a stall for most of your life and taken out only when someone feels like riding you?

Obviously, this is what that person had done as well. WRONG!!! Is that anyway for a house to live?

You know, at lot of people do a lot of things based on own their own sense of what they want or believe they need. Think of all the hoarders in the world. I've known a few. They stock their homes or their businesses with so much unnecessary stuff that is almost unbelievable. Yet, tell them about that fact and they get all defensive. It causes them to live in a state of hell but they are too lost in their own delusion to even realize this fact. Is that anyway to live?

In the case of these fireworks people, who knows why they had all of that stuff illegally stored at their house. It was probably a business or something??? But, what is obvious is by having all that fireworks they put other people, other animals, and other people's property and possessions in danger. They obviously did not think or care about anyone but themselves.

I am sure they did not anticipate or hope for the fireworks to explode in the grand manner that they did. But, nonetheless, simply by owning that kind of stuff it was obvious that something like that could happen. Thus, the owners thought of no one but themselves. Is that anyway to live?

Some people allow themselves to be controlled by their demons. I mean, who else's fault is it when negative Life Things come to control a person's existence. The problem is, those people who are controlled by their demons are generally too lost in their self-thought and addiction to even realize or care about what is taking place; what it is doing themselves and what it is doing to others. Is that anyway to live?

How about you? Are you controlled by your demons? Are your weird idiosyncrasies in control of your life: what you do, and how you think about and behave towards others? If you are, is that anyway to live?

Defined by our individual life circumstance, we can each decide how we should live. Defined by our own mental attitude, we each decide how we take other people and other life forms into consideration. The person who only thinks about themselves: what they have, what they want, what they need, and what they possess is lost to a life defined by Self-ish-ness. If it is, is that you? Is that anyway to live your life?

No Footprints in the Sand
14/Mar/2021 05:21 PM

As you pass through your life, it is defined by doing. Your life is defined by what you have done, what you hope to do, what you are currently doing, and the impact your doing has had on others.

If you look backwards onto your pathway, what have you done? Hindsight is 20/20, so seeing the things you have done is much easier that anticipating what you will do.

What have you done? Do you ever take the time to study the path you have walked?

Many people are so focused on the dreams of their future they never look to what they have left in their wake.

Many people are so lost into the drug of the moment of doing; whatever it is they are doing: loving it or hating it, that they never study the imprinted trail that they have fashioned.

Most people live in a state of oblivion. Yes, they may love or they may hate what they are living at any given moment of their life, but they are not doing anything that they do consciously—nor are they thinking anything that they are thinking consciously. They are simply in a state of objectifying their moment with no thought of how that moment is truly being lived.

Think about your own life, how much of each moment do you truly experience? How much of what you do in each moment is a pathway to a suchness of understanding and helping and how much of what you do is simply an action designed to fulfill what you hope to accomplish, what you hope to become, or how you hope to be perceived?

Every step you take in your life leaves an imprint in the sand. Every thought you think, every word you speak, every act you complete not only affects your own life, your own karma, your own destiny, but it also affects all of the individuals it affects and they thereby affect the person they affect by what they do based upon the waves you have instigated. Thus, as I always say, every person possesses the ability to affect the entire world by what they do; from one person onto the next and the next. But, few ever contemplate this. They just do what they do to get whatever it is they want at any specific moment; at any specific point in their life. How about you?

You have a choice in life; you can do what you do with a very deliberate, defined, and righteous purpose or you can just do what you for yourself defined by whatever whim you are experiencing.

The pathway you carve in life can always be well perceived by anyone who chooses to have the eyes to see it. But, most people simply look the other way. How about you?

All life is your choice. All action you do shapes a pathway. At the end of your days, what will the pathway you are currently living say about you?

I always find it interesting how people post photos from times gone past on places like Instagram, Facebook, and the like. I mean, you get to see a moment captured in time that is no more. That's great! In fact, I love photographs. I always have.

I always had an eye or at least the mind to take photographs. I got my first Kinda Good 35mm camera when I was in junior high school.

Though initially, as we are all inadvertently trained, taking photographs was all about the snapshot. Capturing one of those stupid Fake Smile moments when a couple of people or a family has come together. But, I quickly moved away from that. I wanted to grab the more abstract.

The thing was, and particularly based upon the lifestyle I was living: that of the Non-Attached, Everything is Perfect, Live Only in the Moment kind of stuff, I rarely had my camera with me so a lot of moments were lost. It is not like it is today, with a great camera on your phone that takes better pictures than most 35mm cameras did back in the day. Now, everybody photographs everything. And, this is not a bad thing.

When Eddy Van Halen past away recently, I saw a photo post from Nuno Bettencourt where he said, in essence, this was the only photo he had of Eddy and himself as everybody was far more into living in the moment back then and didn't really think about taking photos all the time as is the case today. That is so true. We/I lived in the moment. I did what I did. We did what we did. But, so much of it was not captured on film.

I follow the Swami Satchidananda account on Instagram. I mean, he was one of my teachers. They post historic photos of him most every day. In one, I even saw myself. That was cool. The thing is, I was around him a lot. I spend time at his home in Montecito, I did the sound for his lectures, I would go to the very small private Satsangs on Saturday night at the Santa Barbara ashram. I did all of this without taking my camera. I never took a Selfie with him. We just didn't/couldn't really do that kind of stuff back then. So, all of those moments are lost to the photo viewing world; left only to my mind, as is the case with so many others of you, and your life experiences.

As mentioned, the people that are running the Swami Satchidananda account on Instgram post a photo most everyday. But, I think to how many other photos there must be of the man out there and the people that surrounded him. I remember there was this one professional photographer who used to take pictures of him and the people at the L.A. *Integral Yoga Institute* all the time. Good guy. I really liked him. Whatever happened to him, I have no idea. But, if he is still alive, and he kept all the negatives, he has a lot of photos of Gurudev and his peeps.

But again, as they are not out there; they are lost to the winds of time. They are not out there for those of us who remember those photographed moments to reminisce over.

So, where does this leave us? Does a photograph make that remembered moment any more real? Yeah, kinda. It, at least, documented and recorded that moment of time for others to see and maybe (perhaps) come to understand. But, photographed or not, a moment lived is a moment lived. At least we have that image in our mind. At least we have it there until we are no more. Then, I guess, the all and the everything of the unphotographed becomes lost to the hands of time.

*　　*　　*

11/Mar/2021 02:32 PM

What does doing something mean to you?

I was going through and organizing some of the magazines that I had written articles for the other day. I got to the 1993 section and there were two magazines, next to each other, that I was on the cover of. Obviously, I've written tons and tons of articles about the martial arts but it was right around this time period that I began receiving a lot of requests for articles from the editors of the magazines so my output truly increased.

I'd only previously written a couple of articles for the magazine I was on the cover of. Nonetheless, they brought me in and had their photographer do the cover shoot. I was excited.

Additionally, I was newly entered into the movie game. I had some minor success in the A-market but it was at the point that I got into the indie game that my career notoriety really took off. At that time, there were a lot of upstart magazines dedicated to the B-Market. This one editor liked some of my films so I sent him a few 8 X 10 photos for my just released Zen Film, *Samurai Vampire Bikers from Hell.* One of the photos I sent him was of this very classic movie star style looking woman, who I had discovered, Tipsy La Fabula. Great girl! I thought for sure if he used any of the photos I sent him he would use that one. But no, when I got the mag my friend and co-star Kenneth H. Kim and I were on the cover. Interestingly, he was also the guy on the cover of *Inside Taekwondo* with me.

FYI: You can check these magazine covers out on this website if you feel like it. I've also posted them to Instagram today.

Anyway, though shocked, I was happy to see my face on the cover. Though, in truth, I'm not a big fan of either of those photographs. But more importantly, it was like my first year in the game; my rookie card. I thought/hoped this kind of front cover coverage was going to go on forever.

As I moved farther into the game, I begin to see the politics that came into play. There were a lot of personal preferences; individually decided likes and dislikes—plus a lot of decisions based on ego. You can't fight that kind of stuff when you're just a player on the field. You can try to influence the outcome of the game but if you're not on the inside, and loved by all, then you are left to playing by someone else's rules.

The one editor, and his martial art magazine, soon left the game—as the dawning of the new era of the internet was taking hold. The other magazine also faded away for the same reason. Time went on, fewer and fewer and fewer magazines were published. Though I got a few more cover shots over the years, it was never what I had hoped for.

You know... This is the reality of life and the truth about the all and the everything... If you are in control of your own whatever, you are in control of it. The moment you step outside of that control zone, however, you lose more and more control with every step you take.

So, this becomes the paradox of life, especially for those who hope to find success. Success is always based upon someone else's definition of your worthiness. It is not based upon what you believe to be your talent or your ability.

What does this leave us with? If you try, you may succeed. Maybe... If you don't try, however, you can't succeed. No way... But, if you do succeed, it will always be highly based upon someone else's appraisal of you. They will decide if you should be on the cover of the magazine, they will decided if you should be read, listened to, or viewed. Thus, success is never based on your true ability—it is not predicated upon the ability or the talent that you believe you possess. At best, it is solely defined if someone else deems you worthy.

As you walk through life, keep this mind. Your success is based upon what someone else believes that you bring or give to their life. If they like what you give, they will give you something. If they don't, then you're left out in the rain all alone like Burt Lancaster's character in the film, *The Swimmer.*

11/Mar/2021 10:02 AM

If it is completely dark do you need to wear your glasses?

The Projection of Your Expectations
10/Mar/2021 09:28 AM

I had an interesting flashback the other day. It was all based in the fact that a couple of weeks ago I came home to find that a young girl had run into my car that was parked in front of where I live. Lucky it had just happened when I arrived or she may have been in the wind. She claimed it was due to her missing the brake pedal. Maybe... My guess is she was texting. But, whatever... Nonetheless I had to take my car to the body shop, have it repaired, and deal with all of that kind of stuff no one really wants to deal with...

Anyway, I had just got my car back. I was in a parking lot walking towards it and I remembered this situation that took place with a friend of mine back in the 1970s.

Back then, for all of us who walked the spiritual path, we did all kinds of weird things to experience life, get in touch with nature, and bring us to a closer harmony with Self and Reality. In any case, he and a couple of his friends had headed up to Oregon to pick apples. I was still in high school or I may have gone along, as well. The difference between him and I was that I was already closely aligned with Swami Satchidananda and the *Integral Yoga Institute,* so I had a home. Plus, picking apples never really appealed that much to me anyway...

In any case, they set off in his car. Apparently, his friend was driving it one night and ran into a guardrail on the highway. When they had finished their mission, they got back to L.A., and my friend expected his friend to fix the damage. My first thought was that is kind of uncaring and egocentric. I mean, they were on a mission together and sometimes shit happens. I mean, I had a friend run into my motorcycle one time with his bike when we were on Sunset Blvd. I never expected him to pay to replace the gas tank on my bike that got damaged.

Anyway, a short time later my friend went off to Central America, as there as apparently some spirituality going on down there. He left his friend a new after-market fender and expected his car repaired when he returned. He returned and nada. His friend hadn't done anything. Then, as in my moment of flashback, I thought, *"How could you expect your friend to know how to remove a damaged front fender and replace it with a new one? I wouldn't know how to do that. I don't think most people would."* Yet, this man had his expectation—as unrealistic as these expectations may have been. In fact, he was quite incensed that his friend had done nothing.

This is the thing about life and about expectations; people project their expectation onto others. They project these expectations onto others and few ever consider if they are realistic or not. Few ever consider if the other individual even possesses the physical abilities or the emotional comprehension to get the expectation accomplished.

Think about your own life, what do you expect from others? What have you expected from others? What have you done and how have you behaved when other people have or have not lived up to your expectations?

How you relate to others—what you expect from others—how you behave when others either do or do not give you what you expect will come to be one the primary definition of your life.

If you expect nothing, you are free. If you expect nothing, then the other person is also free. But, if you expect something, all you have done is to set a never-ending path of satisfactions and/or disappointments into motion. You have also set a pattern of elation or guilt onto the life of someone else. Thus, whatever you expect sets a continuous corridor of karma into motion. Again, if you expect nothing everything and everyone becomes free.

Do you want to be free? If you do, then hold no expectations.

La vida es un proceso paso a paso. Antes no sabias lo que sabes ahora porque entonces no estabas preparado para saberlo. Mira tu vida como un trayecto global. No mires atrás con remordimiento, porque no puedes hacer nada para cambiar el pasado. No vivas pensando en el futuro. Haz algo o no lo hagas. Vive las cosas cuando lleguen... *"El pequeño libro del Tiempo"*

07/Mar/2021 07:45 AM

Sin esa experiencia negativa inicial, no habrías avanzado nunca hacia algo positivo.

Ama todo lo que existe en este momento y serás libre.

07/Mar/2021 07:16 AM

Whenever you hear about someone famous that has died, think about how many emotions that are felt. What about all of the people who die and no one knows their name; shouldn't you feel some emotion for them?

05/Mar/2021 03:09 PM

Live all of life as a new experience and you will be free. Free from worry. Free from expectation. Free from previously gained understandings. Free from earlier experiences that hold you bound to the positive or negative aspects of other people or external events. Let everything in life be NEW.

I noticed this quote from one of my books on Instagram. I think it is from *About Peace*.

I've written so much stuff sometimes I don't remember what I wrote that specific something for…

*   *   *

05/Mar/2021 11:04 AM

Olvídate de intentar comprender todos los acontecimientos de la vida y serás mil veces más Feliz.

I received an interesting email from a man who is sixty years old and lives in Detroit who is interested in learning self-defense applications with the cane to protect himself and possibly protect his dog from attacking hounds, as well. As the man had never trained in the martial arts and had read an article I wrote where I stated that the Hapkido Cane should only be taught to advanced students of the art he was curious if I had any suggestions about where he could gain some additional information because as he put it, *"Cane defense information online is crap."*

Interesting question. It set me to thinking. So, I thought I would answer it here so that other people who have wondered about Hapkido Cane techniques may gain some insight.

To tell my story of training with the cane… When I begin training in Hapkido, in 1964, the art was taught, at least to me, in its purest, most original, form. There was no weapons training at all. It was all about hand techniques, throws, deflections, punches, and kicks. It was not until I begin working with my third instructor, in the 1970s, that I was exposed to Hapkido weapon's training. I was already a black belt. I operated a studio with the man, who had just arrived from South Korea, so he was much more in tune with the new techniques being embraced in the art in Korea at that time. He taught me swords, (Kumdo), the short staff, and the cane. I had already been practicing, on my own, with the long staff and, of course, the nunchaku, which had become somewhat of cultural phenomena in my late childhood and early teen years.

As we ran a school together, we begin teaching weapons to our students at the blue belt level. We felt that was an appropriate time, as they would then possess enough experience to understand the fundaments of body movement in association with a weapon. We would begin by training them with the long and the short staff as these weapons truly teach body/mind coordination. At the red belt level we would then begin their training with sword forms and cane self-defense techniques. As the movement associated with these weapons is much more advanced, we felt it was at the red belt level that the student could actually understand the subtlety of the physical movement necessary to operate these weapons from a refined perspective. Thus, as a teacher, I always felt it took at least a year of training for a student to actual comprehend weapons such as the Hapkido Cane with a cultivated understanding.

All this being said, a weapon is a weapon is a weapon. And, anything can become a weapon. Any item you garb can become a useful weapon to defend yourself if necessary. This is also true with the Hapkido Cane.

The cane is an ideal weapon for the trained or the untrained individual. All you have to do is swing it and it can become your weapon of self-defense. Though this is the case with the cane, as with any weapon, a refined understanding of how the weapon most ideal works, in association with how it best can be used in association with the body, helps in any applied self-defense application.

The reason I believe that training in the fighting arts is important is that what they provide any practitioner with is an understanding of physical combat. Though combat in the studio may be limited to sterile sparing, physically interacting with a supposed opponent trains the body and the mind in how to remain calm during combat and react with precision. This is why I still believe receiving at least basic training is the fighting arts is something anyone should do if they hope to be a proficient self-defense technician. But, as in the case with the person who emailed me, this may not always be possible. Thus, any weapon one decides to employee, as a means of protection, must be understood as best a possible.

As stated, the cane is a very natural weapon. One moment you can be using it to aid in your walking and the next moment, if you are attacked, it can be swung at an opponent. But, how do you swing it?

Wildly swinging any weapon leads to limited results. Yes, you may get lucky and hurt your opponent. But, maybe not. It may only infuriate them. Thus, to understand self-defense with the cane, you need to study its self-defense applications.

I really need to say this... Hapkido Cane self-defense should really be precisely studied over a long period of time as its self-defense applications are very subtle. In a pinch however, you simply need to understand the three elements of the cane that I discuss in the article I believe the gentleman has read. Here's a link to it, The Hapkido Cane. There, you can find out a lot more precise information about the Hapkido Cane and its usage.

The three elements are:
1. The Length of the cane
2. The Shaft of the cane
3. The Hooking Handle of the cane

In brief: The length of the cane gives you the ability to strike out at an opponent. The shaft of the cane can be used by the untrained user as a striking weapon. The hooking handle allows the person to not only maintain control of the cane but can be directed toward the attacker as a stronger, larger striking weapon. In addition, due to the fact that the length of the cane give you distance between your attacker and yourself, be it a person or a dog, simply by bringing the cane up and jabbing it into your opponent, you can use the tip of the cane to strike your opponent multiple times in a rapid manner.

The main thing to kept in mind, whenever you plan to use anything as a weapon is, whatever weapon you choose, it is only as effective as your ability to use it in a precise manner. Thus, whether you are a long trained martial artists or a novice, you need to practice with whatever weapon you plan to employee. Meaning, yes, you can use anything as a weapon, but if you hope to use it effectively, you need to know how it moves and how it feels. Thus, if you want to develop the ability to use a cane as a weapon of self-defense: practice, practice, practice. Swing it in the air. Strike at objects. Experience how impact feels with the cane. Come to understand how you can best use it as an effective weapon of self-defense. Imagine opponents coming at you via various means. Develop the ability, in your mind, to understand how to best use the cane in each of those imagined attack scenarios.

Though I suggest everyone, who hopes to become a competent self-defense technician, train under the guidance of a qualified instructor, this may not always be possible. If this is the case, and you hope to protect yourself with any specific weapon, the only way it can become truly effective is if you understand its mechanics. Meaning, you've got to practice with it. From this, you will hopefully come to understand how the cane, or any other object, can become your ideal tool of self-defense.

05/Mar/2021 07:21 AM

Moments before you die you will certainly have expansive realizations about your life and death but you won't be able to tell anyone.

You Know, There's Other People in This World
04/Mar/2021 03:28 PM

I went to the supermarket this morning. As I was leaving, this lady in her Mercedes stops right in the middle of the exit driveway. I was about the third car behind her in line. She just stopped. Finally, I honked. The lady, a middle-aged woman of Middle Eastern descent, then gets out of her car and slowly walks around it and opens and then closes her passenger door. I guess it was not closed all the way. She then slowly walks back to the driver's side and gets in. The line of cars behind me grows, as there is no way to go around her. Though she's back in her car, she doesn't immediately drive away. What she's doing in there, I don't know? Other people begin to honk. Finally, she slowly drives onward. I wanted to scream, *"You know, there's other people in this world!"*

I always find the way a person drives, the things they do behind the wheel, and the way they behave behind the wheel truly expresses a lot about their interpretation of the world and its people. I mean, just watch people as you drive, you will witness and come into contact with all kinds of behavior.

Now, most people are not as rude as this lady. I would never have done what she did. If I were forced to do something like that, I would have done it triple time. But, this woman obviously cares, considers, or thinks about no one but herself.

When you drive, how do you behave towards other drivers? As you live, how do you behave toward other human beings? Do you think about them first or do you think about yourself first? This is a really important question to ask yourself and to analyze in your mind. Because it will truly reveal a lot about yourself and how others will ultimately come to define you.

Do you think about others? Do you care what your actions may do to them and how your actions will affect another person's life? If you do not think about the other person first and only care about and do for yourself, or even worse make up lies and excuses about how what you do has not affected the life of someone else, you may want to reconsider your behave as you are more than likely unleashing a lot of damage, which may ultimately come to be the definition of your life.

Recently, here in the L.A. area, there were two African-American men surfing in Manhattan Beach. Some Caucasian guy paddled over to them and began insulting them and calling them the, *"N-word,"* over and over again. Bad! Other surfers apparently joined in. BAD, BAD, BAD!

Now, surfers and surfing has always been defined by a very macho, *"Locals Only,"* mindset. In fact, some of the earliest elements of the Punk Rock scene here in L.A. and OC came to be highly defined by surf and skate culture. What should be a very spiritually based expression of human interaction with nature is often marred by bad behave, like the Manhattan Beach incident. Luckily, much of the confrontation was caught on camera by someone on the shore and posted online.

But, is the guy screaming racial profanities sorry? I would guess not. He is more than likely locked into a mindset of, *"Me."*

Here lies the problem with only thinking about yourself, doing for yourself, and not caring about the anyone else; lives get damaged. And, it is rare that the two young men can come out of a damaging experience like this and make something positive out of it as they have.

Why is there is anything wrong with being an African-American surfer? Why is there anything wrong with anyone doing anything that they want to do, as long as it harms no one else?

Wrongness is defined by one person, (or more coming together), and doing something that hurts the life of someone.

Now, the lady in the car today, and perhaps even the racist surfer, are very small pieces in the puzzle of life. These situations will most likely soon be forgotten. But, the action(s) of one person, and the choices they make to perform that action, no matter what their reasoning or justification may be, has the potential to truly alter the life path of someone else. And, this may happen without the instigator ever knowing or caring about how they have hurt the life of that someone else.

The answer, care about people. Care enough to contemplate how what you do will affect the life of the anyone else. Think about the other person first.

In each of our lives there are those people who guide us to become what we ultimately become. In some cases, these people are far off messengers. Maybe we have read their written words, heard them speak via some pre-recorded method, or listened to tales told about them. Then, there is the teacher. The person we interact with face-to-face. Though we can learn from both of these sources, it is only when we personally know our teacher can a direct transmission of knowledge be passed from them to us.

The influencer, the person out there, is held in a place of regard. This regard may be well deserved or it may be based in a false presentation of Self. If you don't personally know the person, you don't personally know them. If you don't personally know the person, you can never truly see their flaws.

No person is perfect, though some people do project the definition of perfection to the world. The reason this projection of perfection is so commonly attributed to a person, as in the case of the influencer, is that individual is off there in the distant: the way they supposedly live their life; the things they say and they do seem so idealistic. But, any thing that is not personally experienced is only an illusion. If it is not personally known, then it is not personally known.

Interaction with a true teacher is, however, based upon experience. It is based upon you being in their presence and witnessing who and what they truly are. Though they may obviously possess flaws, though they may obviously have faults, though they may say the wrong word or do the wrong thing every now and then, by witnessing this and still accepting them as a teacher you can come to understand the true reality of reality.

Knowledge passed secondhand is never true knowledge. Though you may gain understanding by reading a book—though you may find your own realizations from something you read or you heard, but without the personal passage of knowledge, understanding is left to subjective realization, which is most commonly simply based upon ego and not a true understanding of actuality, *"I know! You do not."* This is why there are so many false prophets in the world—people who decide that they know, take to the pulpit, but have never truly passed through the process of direct learning from a true master of the subject.

Ask yourself, *"What do you know and why do you know it?" "What do you believe and why do you believe it?" "From who have you learned what you know and how did they pass that knowledge onto you?"*

If you don't know, you don't know. But, how many people think they know—how many people proclaim they know but when questioned they hold no true transmission of knowledge from a greater source?

People are people, they each possess their own individualized flaws. But, if you are not close enough to a teacher to observe their individualized flaws, you were not close enough to learn from them.

Know your teachers. Know the source of your knowledge. Experience the good and bad, from this you may truly claim to possess a basis of understanding.

*　　*　　*

What happens when both you and a person you don't like find yourself in heaven?

It is very hard not to be confronted with the fact that everyone is evaluating everyone else's life in this time and in this era. Born in the #metoo, #cancelculture, #blm, and #woke movements, people are casting their judgment onto others on a daily basis. But, there is one thing that people do not realize as they are casting their judgment onto to others... That one thing is, looking to others— focusing on others, removes the focus from one's self. Meaning, by looking outwards, no one is looking inwards.

The fact is, it is very easy to look to the life of someone else and see what you do or do not like about the way they have lived their life and the things they have or have not done. But, the one element that no one, *"Else,"* possess is the true understanding of another person's actual inner-motivations for why that person has done what they have done. It is a judgmental guess at best. Again, this is a very easy framework to live your life from as all focus is placed outside of one's self.

Ask yourself, *"Do you truly know what I am thinking?" "Do you truly know what anyone else is thinking?"*

No one likes it when someone accuses him or her of something. No one likes it when someone says something about him or her that is not true. No one likes it when someone falsely judges an individual. But, look around us; it is going on all over the place.

Obviously, this is nothing new in the realms of life and of life reality. What is new, however, is the belief system that everyone immediately places on anything anyone says without doing any true inner-investigation as to if what is being said or claimed is actually fact or self-concocted fiction.

Most recently, they have taken certain Dr. Seuss books off the market due to their racial overtones. Now, this certainly does not affect me in any manner. Even as a child I was not a big fan of Dr. Seuss. I doubt that it affects you. But, what it does illustrate is that the world is in a mode of mass cleansing—eradicating anything that anyone does not believe is appropriate. But, how is this any different than when a new religion takes over a region of the world and burns all of the religious scriptures that were utilized by the original inhabitants? How is this any different than when a new political entity takes over a land and destroys all cultural ruminates of its indigenous people? Destruction is destruction and that is all destruction leads to.

When we look to places like talk radio, the cable news channels, and especially the internet, we see people broadcasting their thoughts and their judgments about all kinds of people and things. But, do these people ever articulate that what they saying is simply what they think about someone or something and what they are stating is not necessarily based in fact? No, they do not. They proclaim what they proclaim as if it is gospel. It is not.

From a personal perspective, people are actually making money on sites like YouTube by discussing movies I have made. Are they paying me anything for having the creative vision and the dedication to get that movie completed? Nope. Are they paying me any money for using the footage from my films to illustrate their discussion? Nope.

105

Does the publicity do me any good? How could it when what they are saying is simply opinion-based wrong? These people don't know me. These people have never met me. These people have never spoken to me. These people have never asked me anything. Yet, they are making money by speaking about my creations, myself, and why they think I do what I do. Is that fair?

Certainly, this type of broadcasting goes on all the time all over the place. Perhaps it has happened to you in some way, so you will understand. The thing is, in this era; opinion, not fact, seems to rule, and who's ever opinion can be voiced in the mode of attack seems to hold the most weight.

If we look to the works of Dr. Seuss, were they intrinsically racists? I don't know. How could I? Was he a racist? Or, as his family proclaims, simply a product of his era? Again, I don't know. You don't know. Nobody knows. Does removing his now seemingly racist illustrations make the all and the everything of the world any better, or does it simply put a veil over a piece of American culture, attempting to hide the facts of a time and a place and an artist's creative vision at a specific point in history?

If we look to the Blaxploitation cinema of the 1960s and 1970s, we can view a lot of reverse racism. The terms they used to speak of Caucasians and other, non-Black, races were very demeaning. I understand that this is considered a form of countermanding the way African-Americans had been spoken of and spoken to in times gone past, but does that type of dialogue truly making anything any better or does it simply accentuate the negative?

I know I've spoken of this before, but growing up in a predominately African-American area of Los Angeles, I was continually confronted with racism. Everyday I was called, *"Honkey,"* or *"White paddy."* Were those people chastised for calling me such derogatory terms? No, they were not as in that sub-culture it was accepted behavior. Did I come back at those people who said such things by calling them a racial slur; no I did not, because that was not of my make up. I just let it roll off my shoulder. I did, from personal experience, however, experientially come to understand that racial slurs do not define the person who they are being aimed at and they have very little actually impact if you do not allow them to dominate your mindset.

I was also confronted with violence, due to my race, on a regular basis. People wanting to fight would often accost me. It was rarely one-on-one but most commonly by multiple people. So, I learned you had to keep swinging no matter what. Now, I'm not playing the, *"Poor little White boy,"* card here. What I am saying is that by judging a person without understanding who they truly are negates all a person truly is. Moreover, playing the, *"Whoa is me,"* card is exactly what most of the people who are out there embracing #cancelculture are doing. They are looking to judging, criticizing, and then attempting to destroy a person, place, or a thing due to their not liking what he, she, or it represents. But, why can't a person be who they are? Why can't they think what they think? And, who is so all-powerful to be the ultimate judge of their thoughts and their actions?

Now many, in this era, feel it is their duty to attack what they deem to be the bad thoughts and actions of other people, and to destroy what they consider to be the bad things of the past. But, destruction does not change anything. It does not alter the past.

In spiritual circles, it is understood that for a person to become truly whole, truly holy, they must focus on themselves and refine themselves first, before they ever venture out to guide others. How many of the people who have taken to the streets, (or the airwaves or the internet), truly spend any time refining themselves, their own inner consciousness, and their own understanding of Divine Self and God? Very few, I believe. Instead, as stated, it is much easy to focus on something outside of themselves. It is much easier to condemn the actions of someone else than to condemn one's own faults and misdeeds.

So, next time you think about criticizing someone, next time you think about discussing someone else that you do not actually know, next time you find yourself placing your analysis, your anger, your angsts, or your condemnation onto someone else, take the time to look at yourself first. What have you done wrong? Who have you hurt? How have you alter the life of someone else, in some manner, by what you have created? And, what are you doing today to truly make yourself, internally, a better and more refined individual?

Judge yourself before you ever judge anyone else. Tell people the truth about who and what you truly are. Be honest with yourself and with others about the things you have done that have affected the life or someone/anyone else. And, always understand that you can never truly know another person so you should never cast your judgment onto them.

One of the most unique things about life is that each person perceives everything via their own distinctive method. What one person may like another person may hate. For example, one person reads a book and finds all kinds of inspiration in the words. Another person reads the same book and is driven to criticism of the words and maybe even the author. Were the words written upon the page any different? No. It was simply one person's perception of what was written on the page.

What this tells us is that everyone operates from his or her own basis of understanding and interpretation of reality. Though we all live in what is understood to be the same reality, each person decodes that reality in his or her own way.

Many people attempt to proclaim that their understanding of everything or anything is more precise that that of anyone/everyone else. These are the people who find their way to the pulpit and present their understandings to the world. But, is their understanding any more precise than yours or is it simply that due their psychological makeup they simply possess the self-centered mindset and the psychological tools to believe that they know more than someone else?

If we look to societies throughout history we see that entire civilization have been based upon religion. This is true, in some cases, even until today. Look to the fundamentalist sects of Christianity and Islam, they place the man in a very dominate role above women. Why is this? Power and control. Look to the cast system that was once strictly employed, and today to a somewhat lessor level, of Hinduism. What was that based upon? Dominance and control.

Some people want to tell other people how they should act and behave. Others are willing to accept this dominance. Why? Because then responsibility is removed. They cannot be held responsible.

This mindset goes to all levels of life. Most people do not want to be at the helm. Most people do not want to be the one who is responsible. Most people wish to be told what to do. This is why churches, temples, and mosques are filled throughout the globe on a daily basis. This is why self-help gurus have so many followers.

In this modern era, many people will deny this fact. But, take a moment and look to your own life. Who are you? What are you? Are you the leader who tells everyone else what you think they should do or are you a follower, listening and responding to your minister, your boss, or someone who pretends to have all of the answers?

If you are a leader, what makes you think that you have any knowledge to give? If you are a follower, why are you willing to listen to the words and follow the suggestions of anyone else?

Take a moment a work this out in your brain.

Everyone has a basis for his or her basis. This fact is based in all kinds of things. This fact leads to all kinds of actions and inactions. But, the one thing that it unquestionably does is to set the stage for a person's life.

Some people are born into this world with a very strong-willed, ego-filled nature. Others are born more passive. Some people are forced to learn how to be a dominant individual. Some are beaten into submission. Whatever the case, each person passes through their life defined by the basis of their basis. Most, however, never question their basis; they never contemplate why they do what they do, why they like what they like, and why they hate what they hate. They simply exist in a state of belief-filled oblivion. But, is that how any life should truly be lived?

Take a moment, define who you are. Look to what you have done and why you have done it. Look to what you do and why you do it. Scan the years of your life.

What are you going to do next? Why are you going to do what you do next? Are you going to broadcast your supposed knowledge to anyone who will listen? Are you going to express your dominance over anyone who will cower? Or, are you simply going to retreat into a state of passive submission, listening to others, being guided by others, and being told what you should or should not believe?

Your life, you basis of basis, your choice.

*   *   *
24/Feb/2021 10:03 AM

What can you do today to make your life better?

What can you do today to make the life of someone you love better?

What can you do today to make the life of someone you don't know better?

What can you do today to undo any hurt you may have caused?

What can you do today to make everybody's everything better?

Will you do it?

*   *   *

What happened yesterday happened yesterday but what happened yesterday sets your today into motion.

There used to be this paper that would come out every Thursday, here in L.A., called the Recycler. It was a paper designed for people to sell and/or to buy pretty much everything. Every Thursday morning I would get up early to get it at this one liquor store where I knew it was delivered early to seek out guitars, synthesizer, and amplifiers. I wasn't the only one doing it; a lot of people were looking for a lot of things.

I purchased a '64 Fender Jaguar from John Sebastian, a '58 Gibson Les Paul from Moon Martin, a Gibson L5-S from Sumner Mering; all well known musicians of the era. Did I know who I was calling up on the telephone? No, I would just call them up, set up a meet time, go to where they lived, check out the guitar, and buy it. All face-to-face.

I also sold things. I bough and sold a lot of guitars and amps via the Recycler back in the day. The guitar player for Slayer showed up at my Hermosa Beach apartment this one time to buy this three rack Anvil case I had designed to hold my three Marshall amp heads back when I was playing live. And, the list goes on and on and on. Tom Petty came over and purchased a Rickenbacker from one of my friends. It was a very face-to-face era. You would go to people's houses or they would come to yours and things were bought and sold.

The nightclubs in L.A. used to be very intimate. I think to this one very popular nightclub, Madam Wong's West. All the great bands of the '80s played there. The thing is/was, it was a very small nightclub. The stage was just set about one foot above the dance floor. So, you would be anywhere from a few inches to several feet away from the performers. Bands such as X, The Plimsouls, 20/20, The Motels, Wall of Voodoo, and Oingo Boingo (who's singer was, of course, Danny Elfman, who went on to be a highly sought after film composer), played there. And, this wasn't the only club in the city like this. There were many. I once saw the Sister's of Mercy at a nightclub in Long Beach that was about the size of my living room. Everyone was face-to-face.

As is always the case, life and times change. Certainly, the internet changed everything. As the internet rolled to power, first things were bought and sold on eBay, which many sites have emulated. I have bought and sold so many guitars and amps, and books, and records, and... on eBay that I cannot even guess at how many. No longer is it a face-to-face transaction. Now, it is some abstract person out there in some far off place that you will never have any personal contact with. There is no personalization.

In fact, pretty much all of the world has become far off and foreign. This has given birth to all kinds of things, many of them negative. Certainly, Troll Culture was born in this realm. The place where people write and speak negatively (or positively) about someone they never met and never will meet. But, how can you truly know anything about anyone if you have actually never met them? Yet, people talk and talk and talk and talk.

Like I have long said, *"You know you're famous when people you've never met say things about you that aren't true."*

The thing is, face-to-face is real. It is a true experience. That experience may be good, bad,

115

positive, or negative but it is real. It did happen. You know what you know because you have lived it. Everything else that is lived in the realm of abstraction, all of this cyberspace mumbo jumbo, is just bullshit. Yet, most people are not personally aware enough to realize this fact. They believe the lie.

In Hinduism, there is the understanding of, *"Maya."* That all of life is an illusion. For the zealot to reach God-Consciousness they must rebuke this illusion and find a pathway to True Knowledge. The fact is, life is only truly known; life is only truly experienced face-to-face. Think about it, when have you truly known what you have known? The answer: When have you truly experienced what you have experienced? When have you actually understood that other person? When? When you were face-to-face.

Now, I could tell everyone to forget all this cyberspace nonsense. But, that is the reality of our time. Some day, this too will change. But, not today. So, what are we left with? We are left with the reality of the reality that we must be strong minded enough to set our own stage for our own reality. We must take control of our lives and our minds and not be forced into mindlessness dominated by all that is not real in the Out There. Or, as in the case of the internet, In Here. We must set the stage for our life to be live in the Real to its fullest. Because nothing is nothing is nothing unless it is something. How does something become Some Thing? When it is lived face-to-face.

Lawrence Ferlinghetti
23/Feb/2021 01:40 PM

Lawrence Ferlinghetti passed away today.

I get it… I imagine that most of the people who read this blog do not know who Lawrence Ferlinghetti was. If you're not into Beat literature and/or modern poetry you may never have heard of him. But, in brief, he was a seminal Beat poet and he founded City Light Publishers and Book Store in San Francisco.

Every time I go to San Francisco I go to City Lights. It's in North Beach and it is a GREAT bookshop.

I had a little bit of a history with Ferlinghetti. Way back, in the way back when, I used to send City Lights my poetry collections in hopes that they would publish my work. A young man's dreams and all of that… It's not like my poetry had not previously been published… Anyway, I guess Ferlinghetti got sick of receiving my stuff. I got a hand written and signed letter from him stating he would never publish me. I guess I should have kept that letter. But, I never keep negative stuff.

But, back then, the 1980s and into the 1990s, they would always have my chapbooks on hand. City Lights has an indie poetry section against one wall and I would always see my stuff being sold there. Whenever I would go in there and see one of my chapbooks I would sign it. So, if you ever see any of those on the market, it was probably signed at City Lights.

But, all this is not the reason I am writing this… A totally bizarre and beyond coincidental thing happened to me this morning. I was looking

117

around eBay and I saw a, *"Bundle,"* of books by Bukowski being sold as, *"Signed."* They were not signed by Buk, as so many books are. FYI: There are millions of his signed books out there. I don't know who signed more books, Buk or Timothy Leary. Anyway, they were being advertised as being signed by Buk's one time girlfriend, Linda King. She signs a lot of his stuff. But, what was not advertised is that two of the books, published by City Lights, were also signed by Ferlinghetti (Editor). I, of course, snapped them up.

I told my lady about it. Not being into poetry, she is also one of those people who didn't know who Ferlinghetti was. ...Though she always goes to City Lights with me. I explained who he was and told her the funny story about his letter of rejection. I also mentioned that he must be very old by this point in time. I looked it up and he was one-hundred and one years old. That was that...

I'm off on my day. As I was driving, listening to NPR, it comes over the airwaves that Lawrence Ferlinghetti had just died today. How bizarre. Just this morning I looked him up and he was still alive. Just this morning I purchased two books that he had signed. Now, he had passed on. I mean that is just coincidence beyond belief. I am so thankful I purchased those books. I think most people could not or would not appreciate the contribution he made to literature. But, I do.

Anyway... If you get a chance and feel like, check out some of his writing. He had a very unique voice. I'm sure you can find a lot of his stuff on-line.

As for literature, another one of the GREATS has been lost. I'm sure there is a poem in all of this but I will save that for someone else to write. This is my tribute. Lawrence Ferlinghetti, thanks for being who you were and doing what you did! And, thanks for the letter of rejection.

Roller Blade Seven:
The Gift That Keeps On Giving
22/Feb/2021 08:39 AM

Have you ever wanted to be in a music video? I know I did. Back in the day, way back in the way back when, when I was focusing my career primarily on acting, I hoped to land a gig as the lead in a music video. As an actor, I got a few small rolls in music videos but never that lead roll I had hoped for. I was offered to play a character in the video for *November Rain* by Guns n' Roses but I thought that would be a little too weird as I used to rent videos from Axel at Tower Records on Sunset and the band used to rehearse at my friend's studio, so I knew them, in that weird way, a little too well so I turned it down. Which, of course, pissed off my agent, as she didn't get her ten percent. A few of my actor friends were in that video, however. Of course, this was back when music videos really set the stage for life…

Very soon after this, Don Jackson and I set about making the first Zen Film, *The Roller Blade Seven*—my life and my career quickly changed as did my filmmaking focus from not only actor to filmmaker. Pretty much from that point forward I have made films, of one type or another, nonstop.

I often speak about how there is virtually never a week that goes by that someone does not ask me some question about *The Roller Blade Seven*. I am also often directed to reviews, mostly criticizing, the movie. Some of my other films like *Samurai Vampire Bikers from Hell, Max Hell Frog Warrior,* and *Guns of El Chupacabra* receive this same treatment but never, at least not yet, as fervently as does *The Roller Blade Seven*. So,

120

whatever we did when we made that film we did something right because thirty years later people are still discussing it.

It's kind of funny, when I woke up this morning I was thinking about writing a piece about the mindset that Don and I possessed while making movies like *The Roller Blade Seven* and *Max Hell Frog Warrior* as still, to this day, no matter how much I have spoken or written about these films, so often the people who speak about them really miss the point—they get so much wrong and they never understand our intentions or motivations.

Anyway, I was planning to write that piece until I was checking my emails and someone pointed me in the direction of a new music video that was just posted using footage from *The Roller Blade Seven.*

I've spoken about this before, but the first band that used footage from RB7, for their music video, was a Scandinavian electronica band back in the '90s. It was good. I never downloaded that video, however, thinking it would be up forever. Unfortunately, it was not. Since then, a couple of bands have used RB7 footage. Some of the music I have liked, others I have not. But, this new video and/or their music is pretty good—good usage of the footage.

I guess I should throw them some props. The band is called Valuemart and the song is called *Born to Kill.* You can find it on YouTube. I also popped up a link to it over on the NEWS page of this website.

I don't know the people in this band—never met them; at least not that I know of. But, I checked them out and their music is good. They also have a page over on Bandcamp. So, check them out if you feel like it.

Kinda funny… My lady was passing by when I was watching the video and I told her about it. She made the joke, *"Why does everybody like thirty-two year old Scott Shaw so much and not sixty-two year old Scott Shaw?"* …Though I think I look pretty much the same. ☺

Anyway, I never really thought about it or consciously realized it until this morning, I guess I finally got to be that lead in music video that I hoped for so many years ago. So, thanks guys!

Life is weird… But, if you don't create, then nothing is created. If Don and I had never made RB7 I might never have become the lead in someone else's music video. So, my advice; create. Maybe you will make your own *Roller Blade Seven* that people will still be talking about and using footage from for their music videos some thirty years later.

So… I was doing the basic restringing, oiling the neck, and intonating one of my 12-string electric guitars. Though the guitar has a great feel and a great tone, it has these kind of weird tuning keys so it takes a bit longer to string than it should. But, anyway… That's not the point.

I was at home so I decided to throw on an LP.

Due to the fact that I am always kind of ON, I really don't have a lot of time to listen to records. That's sad, I think. Most of my music listening is done in the car. Though that's fine, as it suitably fills the time while driving, there is really something GREAT about listening to music on vinyl. I mean, get yourself a good receiver/amplifier and a good turntable, (never use those all in one units as they kill the vinyl), sit back and let the music magic happen. The sound is just so subtly exquisite.

For my listening pleasure this day, I grabbed a couple of my recent thrift store finds. Though I assuredly have a couple copies of most on my albums, when I see something that catches my eye, I grab it. You never know when you'll see it again.

First up was, Pink Floyd, *Meddle*. Though they were certainly a part of my generation, I was never a big fan of Pink Floyd. I gabbed this LP at the thrift store because it was a first pressing in very good condition. I hadn't listened to this LP in decades. Now, as the last time, somewhere back, in the way back when, I wondered is this really Rock or is it something else?

Next up was, Spandau Ballet, *Parade*. As it started to play, I flashed back. As the music played, this LP became a real memory churner. Not because I was a super fan of the band or anything like that but I remember sitting in this café in Bangkok in '84, with my then Thai love, as this LP played over the sound system when this band was at the top of the charts. It's so strange, because nothing was really going on in that situation. We were just sitting there drinking coffee. But, that life situation is one of those memories that stays in your mind for some unknown reason. I think I even wrote a poem about it, published in my book, *Bangkok and the Nights of Drunken Stupor.*

Inspired by the 80s, I finished up my listening by actually going into the collection and pulling out the great album by Regina, *Curiosity;* which has that great-great pop song, *Baby Love* on it.

Life is interesting, we do what we do while we are doing it. We live what we live while we living it. Most of it, just passes us by. Most life THINGS are just life THINGS and we never really think about them. But, maybe we should.

How much music do you listen to and really study? Sure, you like what you like and don't like what you don't like. …You want to hear what you want to hear and don't want to hear what you don't want to hear. Everyone hears music all the time. It's playing everywhere. But, how often do you sit down and really study it? …Truly listen to the notes and the lyrics?

Music is very interesting because it sets the stage for our life. As stated, I remember listening to that album nearly forty years ago in that café in Bangkok. I'm sure you also have moments that you

124

remember, defined by the music you were listening to. But, how much of that music do you (did you) really hear?

I don't know... I could go on and on about this forever... But, my guitar is cleaned up and restrung, so I need to go plug it in and make some music that no one will ever hear.

Victimhood and the Definition of Who You Are
20/Feb/2021 07:21 AM

Recently, there have been a few women that have come out and made serious accusation about their famous ex-boyfriends or ex-husbands. Watching morning TV and even the Dr. Oz Show these women have been featured. I believe this is a very interesting phenomenon for a couple of reasons. Perhaps the most of which is that the only reason that these people are being presented, on the national level, is that they are speaking about someone who is famous. If these women were not speaking about someone who is notable their voices would not even be heard and their accusations would certainly not be broadcast to the world.

Now, there are all kinds of levels of supposition we could go into about why these women are speaking out. There are also all kinds of issues of defamation, (is it true or is it not), that could be contemplated, and as none of us know how any of this is going to turn out I don't want to mention any names, but that is not really the issue. The issue is, how one person claims to be a victim and calls out another person to be the wrongdoer.

The question emerges, is victimhood a good place to be operating from? And, who ultimately is the victim?

It is very obvious, and has been proven throughout history, that the majority of the people who unleash abuse onto others are those who were themselves abused. Abuse is a learned behavior. So yes, one person may be saying or doing something that someone else finds abusive but if we look to the life history of the doer, almost universally, that is how the so-called abuser was taught how to

126

encounter life and how to react to other people. In fact, many times when a person is young their abuser is also proclaiming their love for their victim. From this, the person who later does things that are decreed to be abusive is, in fact, simply acting out on what they believe is an example of love; as distorted as that example may be.

As we see, abuse emanates from a very veiled place in the mind of the so-called abuser. Moreover, abuse comes in many undefined forms and is only called abuse when the receiver deems it as such.

I get it, this is a very controversial issue and many people have very specific ideas about this subject and I'm not trying to piss anyone off. But, if we look to modern society and to the people who have either claimed victimhood or were projected as such, we see that they become defined by that label.

For example, if we step back a few years, when Chris Brown brutally beat up Rihanna everyone assumed his career would be over and perhaps her next boyfriend would take revenge. But, nothing happened. Aside from the minor charge he caught, where he got probation and community service, his career continued to thrive. Art Alexakis, of the band Everclear, detailed how he was sexual assaulted by a group of boys when he was a youngster. In the early days of his band, in the 1990s, this attack seemed to be some sort of misguided marketing tool but to this day, whenever he is interviewed, he is often required to mention that experience. You can see he wants to move pass it but it has become one of the definitions of his life. Thus, victimhood has become his calling card. Is that a good thing?

I am not diminishing any person's claim of abuse nor am I negating any of these experiences as they must have been horrible to have lived through. But, the point being is, why does anyone want victimhood to become the definition of his or her life?

Yes, claiming victimhood, at the hands of someone famous, has propelled certain individuals into the public eye and provided them with a voice and, in some cases, even career advancement. But, at what cost?

This victim mindset is not limited to what one person did to another. During this point in history we are witnessing entire movements based upon victimhood. ...Movements based upon what one race did to another race and/or to what one segment of society, (say the police), did to specific groups of people. Again, this is a tool used to get a message out there but at what cost? What does it cost the individual or an entire race to become defined as a victim?

For many of us, myself include, we have experienced some appalling things delivered to us by the hands of other people. Particularly as children, there is very little we can do about this.

For many of us, myself include, we have done some things that were less than commendable to other people. We can blame the, *"What was done to us,"* but it was, nonetheless, we who did what we did to someone else. We must own that fact and never make excuses for it, especially to ourselves.

All life is interplay of human interactions. We are all formed by what we have experienced. And, we shape the life of others by what we do to them.

For those of us who care, we try to become better people and move away from our Lower Self. We try to learn from our mistakes and fix the things we have broken. For others, they lock themselves into a place of negativity throughout their life. Whether that negativity was given birth to by what someone did to them or not, it was they who chose to embrace it. Meaning, it is ultimately you who has the choice about how you choose to be defined. You can decide to be a victim. You can define your entire life by that moniker if you want to. But, is that who and what you ultimately want to be and/or become? Is that how you want the rest of the world to feel about you? Or, do you want to be the person who overcame your victimizer or victimizers and rose to a place where you were not defined by what was done to you but the good you have done for others?

*　　*　　*

20/Feb/2021 07:02 AM

Who do you love?

What do you love?

Take a few moments and make a list in your mind of the people and the things that you love.

Now that you have this list do something nice for the people and the things that you love.

For the things you love maybe wipe them down, clean them, wash them, or polish them.

For the people that you love, let them know that you love them, do something good for them.

Spend today loving the things you love.

19/Feb/2021 07:19 AM

The good news is, you will most probably forget this moment of your life.

The bad news is, you will most probably forget this moment of your life.

*   *   *

18/Feb/2021 07:46 AM

When does a lie become the truth?

How many times have you done something like eat your lunch but you did not even really taste your food because your mind was on something else?

If you wish to have a fully-experienced life you must embrace each experience to its fullest—you must study and embrace all that you are doing, when you are doing it, to the best of your ability.

You Really Can't Have an Opinion Anymore
16/Feb/2021 09:21 AM

This whole #cancelculture thing has really gotten out of control. It is really pretty scary to watch how the moment one person voices their opinion and their opinion goes against the gain of anyone else all of a sudden they are fired or required to, *"Step down,"* from their job. Certainly, this is most prominent for people who are in front of a camera, in front of a microphone, or are in-print but why can't a person be allowed to think what they think even if it does go against the grain of whatever political correctness that is taking place in whatever current situation? Why does everything everyone thinks and maybe spurts out by mistake have to become a nail in the coffin of their life? Why can you no longer just say what you think and feel? Why can't you have an opinion?

This has been going on for a while now. Just think of all of the people who have been removed from their position because they stated that they understand or approve of something that may have been okay a few years back but is now forbidden. Why can't a person think what they think? And, if a person is hiding what they really think and believe, and covering it up with some falsehood, doesn't that make them a hypocrite? Is that the kind of person who should be okay'ed?

Now, I get it. We are in a time of rapid cultural change. ...At least here in the U.S... And sure, a lot of bad has been done to a lot of people in the past. I'm not taking about any of that. Bad is bad is bad. Don't say or do bad things! What I am talking about is that most of the people who have recently been brought down for their opinion have simply been saying what they think about a subject that perhaps they have not truly thought out. Or maybe, what they say is a completely an innocent off the cuff response to a question they did not expect. It doesn't make them a bad person!

I have watched, in the media particularly, how someone will voice their opinion or make an off-color joke and be gone the next day. You can watch as oftentimes the person asking the question or the person who instigated the conversation takes pride in their having taking that person down. What about that? What about that kind of an attitude? Shouldn't that be a reason for a person to lose their job? But, it's not.

This whole #cancelculture thing is all about attack. It is all about being judgmental. Isn't being like that bad? Shouldn't that style of behavior be criticized?

You know, we are all human beings... We are all created, reared, and indoctrinated where we were schooled in the ways of the world. We were created by our society and by where we found ourselves in our society. We all say or do things that, assuredly, someone else is not going to like. But, attacking on any level, judging on any level only leads to confrontation. And, at the root of all things right in the world, confrontation is wrong. Hurting is wrong.

Does anyone have the right to hurt someone simply because they do not like what they think or say? Does anyone have the right to hurt you simply because of what you think or say?

For all of these people who are in attack mode... For all of these people who want to bring people down... You really should think about what you are actually doing because sooner or later someone is not going to like what you think or say and then it will be you who is brought if we allow this style of behavior to become the norm.

Doing Nothing Verses Experiencing Nothingness
15/Feb/2021 02:41 PM

The term, *"Mu,"* is used in both Japanese and Korean. The term, *"Wu,"* is used in Chinese. This term is used in association with the Buddhist understanding of, *"Nothingness."* But, what is Nothingness? Is it having nothing? Is it doing nothing? Or, is it something much more profound?

In life, most everyone wants to do something. They wish to accomplish somethingness. But, how many of those people who Want to Do actually do anything? Most of the dreams that people hold are expressed only in the fantasies in their mind or in their conversations. People can think and talk a lot about what they want but few take the steps in achieving anything. Fewer still follow through to actualizing their end goal.

Why is this? The fact is, thinking, hoping, and believing is easy, whereas achievement is very hard. This is especially the case when one must have other people either help in their goal of achievement or approve them for the level of achievement they desire.

This is the thing about life and the reality of the reality of life; all things, *"Life,"* requires the doing and the approval of so many people. Many times these people are unknown to the desirer of achievement. Thus, doing becomes a competition of a single person against the reality of life. This is why those who do actually do achieve are so well thought of. They have fought against the tides of life and have won.

But, what does winning, what does achieving actually equal? Does it provide true happiness? Does it provide the perfect life and lifestyle? Does it remove all unhappiness? Does is give the all and the everyone in the world something they actually need? Maybe, but most probably not. Why? Because, *"Doing,"* is based in someone's wanting. They desire that achievement and they set out to accomplish it. By the very definition of this process, all that is known to provide an individual with spiritual emancipation is gone. All that is fulfilled, at best, is the achievement of a desired desire. Thus, all that is given birth to is ego. Is ego helpful to anyone but the person who is feeling it? No. Therefore, by basing your life on, *"Doing,"* you may achieve something, you may even become noted for that achievement, but what truly occurs is that you are ultimately and permanently removed from the higher understanding of the No-Self.

There are those who consciously choose to leave the world and all of its desire(s) behind and focus their attention on the embracing, Mu. There is one problem in this process, however. That problem is, if the achievement of Conscious Nothingness becomes a goal, then it can never truly be experienced. Thus, the basis of its true understanding is lost. It is for this reason that walking the path of desire, no matter how spiritual that pathway may sound to the naïve ears of the uninitiated, if any step that is taken is taken with a goal in mind, the true essence of Nothingness is lost.

All people want. Most people want to achieve. Many people spend their entire life attempting to succeed. But, this is one of the ultimate illusions of life. Accomplishment is never whole and complete onto itself. No matter what you do, no matter what you do accomplish, it will only lead to you wanting/desiring something more.

So, where does this leave us? It leaves us with the understanding that doing can be done; doing may even lead to accomplishment for the life of a very few, but doing can never lead to true peace, true happiness, and divine understanding.

Do you wish to live your life forever unfulfilled? Do you wish to live your life constantly chasing? Do you wish to live your life hoping for and dreaming of something that you may never achieve? If you do, then do. If you don't, if you want that illusive understanding of true inner tranquility, then seek out, Mu. It is there that all of the wants are fulfilled without ever doing anything.

Distracted by Deception
14/Feb/2021 08:41 AM

Have you ever noticed that when you lie to someone, when you deceive them, all of your life, in regard to that relationship, becomes complicated? The thing is, and the reason most people lie and/or deceive another person is that they do not think about this. Even if they have told a lie or unleashed some level of deceit against someone in the past, and suffered the consequences, they put all of that out of their mind, thinking that it will not happen again.

The thing about life is, the moment you instigate some level of dishonesty, all of your life becomes complicated in regards to the person you have deceived. Why? Because you must back up the lie. You must continue the lie. You must find a method to establish the foundations for the lie. With all of this comes complications, anxiety, and fear that the truth will be reveled.

Some people don't care about the truth. They live their whole life based upon a lie. They find methods to foundationally substantiate their lie. Others, tell lies all the time. Even though the may be caught time after time, the foundational construction of their being is that they are a liar. Thus, they are a compulsive liar. Not good. But, that is their reality. But, a person like this can never be trusted. From this, their entire life becomes defined by the lies they tell leading to a world of people who know that they are not a person living within the realms of truth and that all they say is most probably false.

Some people love to hear the lies of others. They wish to believe them. Why? Because that other person's lie is better than any truth that they are living. It is like a movie on the screen; false but an illusive reality that draws the viewer in.

The thing about deceiving someone, no matter what your logic or reasoning, is that what you speak is not the truth. Thus, what actually is the truth must remain hidden. From this, you are cast to a pattern of doing all you can to hide the truth from that individual or individuals that you lied to. Thus, this deception becomes the primary thought whenever you are around that person or persons. What occurs from this is a life defined by the anxiety you will (or at least should) always feel and a fear that the truth will come out. Then what? Then, you will either need to formulate another lie to justify your previous lie or come clean and from this that person you lied to may never forgive you or believe you again.

Think about a lie you have told. Think about how complicated it made your life. Maybe you got away with it and from this you told another and another and another lie. But, the fact always is, a lie is never the truth and even if no one ever find out that you told that lie, that you deceived them—what you said, leading to what you did, is still a deception, it is/it was not based upon the truth of the truth.

From a lie all you are left with is a lie. A lair always encounters other liars, as that is the type of person they attract.

Do you like to be lied to? Probably not. Thus, the simple answer to a lair is, do not lie. Tell the truth. From this, not only will your life become so much less complicated but also you will be trusted. And, isn't that one of the best things that you can be?

*   *   *

What happens when someone gives you that gift you really wanted but the gift turns out to be a nightmare? Who's fault is it; yours for wanting it or theirs for giving it to you?

A bit of family tragedy has just struck…

It was just a couple of weeks ago that my lady and I were discussing that we didn't personally know anyone who had gotten *The Rona* (COVID-19). That was then…

My brother-in-law went out to party with his friends shortly after that discussion and brought it home. He ended up spending three days in the hospitable. He was released and is recovering. That's not the tragedy. The tragedy is, he gave it to his mother; my mother-in-law.

What happened next is that, initially, she went to the emergency room but they sent her home with some meds. She continued to get worse. She was hospitalized about two weeks ago. She kept getting worse, even after giving her Remdesivir, so they intubated her. That's pretty much a death sentence. This evening, they pulled the tubes and she passed away. My brother-in-law killed his own mother.

This, when there are vaccines out there that are ready to go. All these politicians make promises about everyone getting vaccinated. But, unless you are on the inside, it is impossible to get one. Yes, there are vaccines but people are still dying because they can't get vaccinated!

For all of you people out there who don't believe this shit is real, think again. A lot of people have died.

My bother-in-law, he's kind of a dead beat. Forty-four years old and living with his mother. He used to steal cars and stuff. Did time in jail. He keeps meeting nice girls, he gets them pregnant, and then when they find out what kind of person he is, they leave him. Thus, the really sad thing is, the life of his kids have all been ruined.

Now, I understand the foundations for this guy's behavior more than most. As the story goes, his father would actually pull the car over to beat him when he was a kid if he pissed him off while they were driving somewhere. And, that's not even talking about what went on at home. For anyone who knows anything about old-school Korean fathers, this is not unusual behavior. Wrong, but not unusual. Combine that with being the pampered only son and it is/it was a catastrophe in the making.

So, he goes out to party. His friend gave it to him just as his friend gave it to his own family. They apparently all recovered, however. That's good news for them. But, my bother-in-law brought it home and gave it to his mother equaling her death… A death that did not need to happen!

You know, if I had done something so foolish and selfish like that, I don't how if I could live with myself. But, everyone has their own psychology. Most people, especially those who were fucked up in their childhood like he was, they have a strange sensibility. So, how he will ultimately react to this or what he will do, I don't know. I do know, he will now be homeless. He killed his meal ticket. But, the point being, all this didn't have to happen! I mean, the word has been out there forever: don't congregate with people not of your immediate household, don't party, social distance, and wear a face mask. But, how many people listen? One person, for sure, did not. And, look what occurred.

Now, she's gone. Killed by *The Rona.* Killed by a foolish person who preferred not to care or believe that it would be him that got it.

I never called my own parent's, *"Mommy,"* or *"Daddy,"* or anything like that. I always called them by their first names. My mother-in-law, however, everybody always referred to her as, *"Mommy,"* so I called her that, as well. Now, she's gone. Gone for no reason. Gone for a selfish gesture that took another person's life. Murder, by any other name. This style of murder is not illegal, however. But, it should be.

I get it; no one feels anyone else's pain. That's why so few people actually try to live a good life and/or attempt to fix anything that they've broken when they've done something wrong or something that has hurt someone else. I guess that's just the human condition. Moreover, few people care about how another person is feeling. But, it doesn't have to be that way. You can care. You can curb your own actions if they have the potential of hurting (or killing) someone else. You can reach out a helping hand. You can unleash a gesture of love. You can try to make things better and make things right. But, will you?

Think about this situation, it could happen to anyone in these days of the coronavirus. Let it guide you in how you behave.

Be careful. Be safe. Think about the other person. Think about how what you do could actually kill another person. Think about it, because it is happening everyday.

Thoughts of Self Verses Thoughts of Others

Every night before you go to sleep what do you think about? Every morning when you wake up what do you think about?

If you wish to develop a clear understand about the focus of your life and gain a look into who and what you truly are, answering those questions is an ideal technique to help you acquire that understanding.

You can be whatever person you want to be. You can become whatever person you wish to become. The focus of your life is the guiding factor for what you will become.

What do you desire to become? What do you desire to be? What do you think about and when do you think about it as you develop a pathway in your becoming?

For me, every night before I go to sleep I have a mantra I ponder, *"What can I do tomorrow to help someone?"* Every morning when I wake up I ponder the mantra, *"Who can I help today."*

Many times, the answer is small things. I'm not a rich man so I don't have a lot of money to throw around. But, what I do have is the ability to help others, even if this is in some small way. So, each night before I go to sleep I ponder what I can do in the next day to actualize this hope. In the morning I either reinforce what I contemplated the night before or come up with a new idea. In either case, it allows me to set the course of my day(s) in a positive direction of trying, in whatever small way I can, to make the life of other people perhaps just a little bit better.

Your life can be solely focused on you. This is the case for most people. But, it doesn't have to be. You can still be you; you can still become the best version of you while attempting to make the all and the everything of everyone just a little bit better.

Every night before you go to sleep what do you think about? Every morning when you wake up what do you think about?

*   *   *

09/Feb/2021 10:45 AM

If somebody died but you don't know that they're
dead are they still alive in your mind?

Filmmaking Is Not Just About Acting
09/Feb/2021 10:00 AM

Whenever I hear people discussing a film, the first thing that most commonly becomes their focus is the acting. More commonly than not, this is the basis for a person's loving or hating a film. But, filmmaking is about much more than the acting. This is the thing that few people have developed the vision to understand as they evaluate a film.

For anyone who is not a filmmaker, it seems that, when critiquing a film, all they focus upon is the actors. Sure, for a story-driven film, the acting is a central part of the watching experience. For the filmmaker, on the other hand, they understand that so much more goes into creating a film than simply the actors saying their words.

I could go into a long discourse here about all of the things that go into making a film such as the locations, the sets, the props, the costuming, the lights, the cameras, the lenses, the camera angels, the sound, the blocking, not to mention the editing and the soundtrack but until a person has actually experienced what it takes to create all of the elements of a film all they are left with is their opinion about what they are viewing. Thus, what they describe after watching a film is almost completely defined by what they do not personally understand. Moreover, if a person has not been a participant in actually bringing all of the components of a film together, again, they lack any true understanding of what it takes to create a film either on the low or the high budget level. Again, all that is left is their estimation about what they have viewed.

All art is defined in the mind of the viewer. How one analyses art is defined by a person's individualized understanding of art. How much a person has studied and learn about the actual inspiration, creation, and evolution of art highly defines how they will approach any form of art that they see.

So, what does this tell us? It explains that all understanding is defined by what an individual does or does not know. It is framed by a person's ability to see beyond the obvious. It is categorized by what a person is willing to understand. It is delineated by one's desired ability to see beyond the obvious.

There are a million things that go into all elements of a life. Think about your own life. How many things are there that have created who you are? How many thoughts, feelings, and life-actions do you take everyday to create your life-experience. And, how many of those things are only known to you or the people that are close to you? How many of those subtle elements will never be known by the vast masses of the people Out There? Yet, those are the people who view your life and believe they know what is going on with you. But, how can they?

All life is based upon a subtle interplay of the all and the everything. Much of this STUFF is very unseen. Yet, it defines all of our lives.

Watching a movie and then evaluating that movie is an ideal example of how you interpret life. Do you study the subtleties? Do you contemplate the unseen? Or, do you simply cast your judgment based upon what you like or dislike and what you think you know?

All art, all life is a sublet manifestation of a person's personal reality. As no one can really know you, how can you believe you know the subtle reason(s) of anyone else?

Allow all things to be as they are and you are free. Allow all things to exist in their own perfection and all is well with the world. Judge and all you have provided is an unsubstantiated opinion. What does that leave the world with? Nothing more than the fact that you have proven that you do not know what you are taking about.

*   *   *

08/Feb/2021 09:48 AM

Instead of taking the easy road of blaming someone else why don't you take the harder, more truthful path and blame yourself?

There is a couple of way to translate the word, *"Discipline,"* from English into Sanskrit, depending on how it is to be used. A couple of the most common words are, *"Abhyāsa," "Niyana," "Anunaya," "Vinaya,"* or, *"Manovinayana."* Perhaps the most direct way of translating this concept into English is the word, *"Caryācaraṇa,"* which refers to the practice of self-discipline.

Yoga is a pathway of discipline. Whereas most people when they hear the term, *"Yoga,"* simply think of it as the physical postures that people perform. This, however, is a very small part of the overall understanding of yoga. The Sanskrit term, *"Yoga,"* literally translates as, *"Union with God."* But, what does this actually mean?

The thing that many practitioners of modern yoga do not understand is that the yoga they do in their classes is properly defined as, *"Hatha Yoga."* This yoga is a small part of the greater overall understand of, Raja Yoga. Raja Yoga is a pathway of mental and physical disciple that leads the practitioner towards communion with God. But again, what does this actually mean?

Yoga is a practice based in Hinduism. Though many people wish to disassociate the physical postures they preform in their classes from this fact, this is the fact. Yoga is a Hindu-based practice of mental and physical purification. I cannot tell you how many devoutly practicing Christians, who practice Hatha Yoga, I have mentioned this to and they go into complete denial about this fact. They make up all kinds of mental excuses. But, there is no denying the birthplace, the evolution, and the true meaning of yoga. It is based in the Hindu understanding of reality.

This is not a good or a bad thing. This is just a thing. But, for so many people who base their entire reality upon their Western-based religion, such as Christianity, the path they walk by preforming yoga, is in direct conflict with their chosen beliefs.

For the most part, Christians do not base their life upon following a disciplined existence. Thus, the concept of focusing their existence on the concept of restraint is alien to them. But, discipline is at the heart of all practices and all forms of yoga. Even the Tantric Yogis of Khajuraho perform their techniques based upon self-discipline.

"Pariṣkāra," translates as, *"Self-discipline."* This understanding is at the heart of all yoga practices. But, how many people who perform the modern applications of Hatha Yoga or pranayama, *"Breath Control,"* ever even contemplate the root of what they are doing? They just do. And, here lies the problem with the modern, undisciplined practice of yoga. It entirely misses the point.

You can go to any exercise class and hopefully get your body in better shape. The Western purveyors of modern, *"Yoga,"* make all kinds of claims about its benefits. And yes, there are many. But, if the essence of, *"Yoga,"* is not embraced and understood how can there be any true internal growth via its practice? If people live in denial about what, *"Yoga,"* truly is, how can they actually live what it has to offer.

Yoga is based in discipline. It is based in self-discipline. It is based in a prescribed control of the body and the mind designed to bring the practitioner closer to physical understanding leading to spiritual awareness. Is yoga a practice based in Christianity or any other Western religion? No, it is not. It is based in an understanding formulated in India thousands of years ago.

Can yoga be adapted to practitioners of other religions? The answer to that is yes and no. Yes, the physical postures can be performed and maybe they will help the health of the practitioner. But, without a true emersion into what, *"Yoga,"* truly is, the absolute essence of this religious-based practice is lost. Thus, the answer is also, no.

Yoga is a religion. It is a part of a religion designed to guide the practitioner towards spiritual growth via discipline. If you are not willing to see, *"Yoga,"* for what it truly is and accept is foundations, then, at best, all you are doing when you practice, *"Hatha Yoga,"* is getting your body more stretched while living in denial about what you are actually doing.

The essence of yoga is, *"Union with God."* How do you achieve that? Discipline. How do you not achieve that? Pretending that you are doing something while not understanding what is actually taking place.

Don't lie to yourself. Yoga is a religion. It is a religion based in Hinduism. If you're not willing to become a Hindu then you can't really practice true, *"Yoga."*

How Old Do You Have To Be?
05/Feb/2021 09:33 AM

I was watching a local morning TV show this AM. The show did a segment on a sixteen-year-old girl who was a certified yoga instructor. They were making a big deal about how she was the only one ever... But, that's not true. I was a certified yoga instructor at sixteen and I am sure there were those, at that age, that came before me and after me. But, I get it, it was a hype piece. And yes, that is pretty cool that the girl is a young yoga instructor. But, there are a lot of people that do a lot of things when they're young. I think one of the big problems with life is, so many people are held back from accomplishing things when they are young all based on their age. From this, a lot of young people are driven away from truly accomplishing; for when you are young you have the time, the desire, and the motivation to achieve your dream but, if you are stopped from doing that, defined solely by your age, then what is anyone left with? A life possibly lived unfulfilled.

Certainly, (for whatever karmic reason), I became involved with the martial arts and with Eastern Stuff like Hatha Yoga when I was very young. I guess that's a good thing??? It certainly came to define my life. I mean, I earned my black belt before I was even a teenager. This was before someone came up with, what I considered to be a very stupid idea, of only awarding junior black belts to those people who are under the age of eighteen. If you earned it, you earned it!

Back then, things were very different. No one gave out black belt diplomas or anything like that. Though I was formally teaching the martial

156

arts by the age of like thirteen or fourteen, as an assistant instructor, (or whatever you want to call that position), nobody ever gave me a diploma stating that fact, like seemingly everybody must have today. It was just understood that I knew my stuff and I could teach.

The story told of the young yoga instructor is that she and her mother looked for several years for someone who would allow a teenage girl to take a yoga instructor's training program. Finally, she found one. They showed her certificate but I've never even heard of the organization that awarded it. So, what does that certificate mean? Back when I first became involved with Eastern Thought and offshoots like Hatha Yoga, no one ever asked me my age. I was just allowed to be who and what I was. By seventeen, I was helping at full-on Yoga Retreats. Though all of the retreat leaders knew my age, they did not define me by my age.

By twenty-one, when I was a martial arts school owner, I used to hate it when sixteen or seventeen years old potential students would come in to sign up and I would have to tell them they had to get their parents to sign their release form as they were not legally an adult. In their mind, they were. In my mind, as well. But, the law is the law is the law.

Back in my day, no one ever asked me (or my parents) to sign anything. If they had, they may have really turned me off and made me walk a different life path. But, I was simply allowed to be and to learn what I was ready to learn.

So, want does this tell us? It tells us that life, that the people of life, wish to take command over the life of others. They may wish to do this by defining a person by their age or by the certificates they were allowed to earn. What it does not allow is a person to be whatever it is they truly are, wherever they may find themselves in the pathway of their life.

You hear a lot about how there is age discrimination for the elderly. For the young, however, it just has become all so expected. *"You're too young to do that?"* Why? Why is anyone too young to do what they have the desire to do? Why is anyone too young to accomplish what they desire to accomplish; no matter how old they are?

So, as you pass through life, think about this. As you meet and interact with other people, think about this. Think about how you judge a person based upon their age. Think about what they are kept from achieving simply because of their age. Remember what you may have been kept from accomplishing based upon your age.

Life is a pathway of accomplishments. If you stop someone from accomplishing, for whatever reason, you may have truly robbed the world from the true gift(s) that they had to provide humanity.

Stayin' When You Should'd Been Leavin'
04/Feb/2021 08:33 AM

"Let he who is without sin among you be the first to cast a stone at her." John 8:7

Ever since the dawn of the #metoo movement and later #cancelculture a lot of accusations have been flying all over the place. I've written about this a few times over the past couple of years and have discussed some of the repercussions. A lot of people have been making a lot of claims. The key factor in all of this is that someone is calling someone else out for what they believe was their wrongdoings. Okay...

Now, I'm not going to go into the fact that a lot of these accusers have also been proven to be none too pure in all of their dealings with others people. But, who hasn't? Who is perfectly pure and has done nothing wrong?

One of the key factors I find in all of this Calling Out is one person is blaming another person for what they did to them while they were in some sort of relationship with that person—however that relationship may have been defined. Here's my question, *"Why didn't you just leave?"*

Sure, there are some very bad situations where one person holds another person against their will. That's flat out wrong. But, in most of these flying accusations, it is defined by one person staying with a person when they should have just left. If they had left, none of the bad would have been allowed to occur.

If you find out a person is a bad, leave. Communicate with them no more. For if you stay, then you have become part of the problem. You have feed the situation. You have become a willing participant in whatever is going on.

It is easy to look back through time and blame someone else for something. I know I have people I look back at and have less than ideal thoughts about based on what they did to me. But, who can I blame but myself for letting that person into my life? Sure, they may have lied to me. Sure, they may have deceived me. Sure, they may have cheated me. Sure, they may have hurt me in some way, shape, or form. But, if I had not chosen to drink the Kool-Aid none of that anything would have happened. And, I imagine some people feel that way about me. I'm no saint.

The main thing about life is, it is easy to throw blame at that someone else. The much harder thing about life is to blame yourself. But, if you choose to willingly interact with anyone for any reason, you are as much to blame for any negative event that takes place as that person you are pointing your finger at.

Your life is your fault. Who is really to blame?

*   *   *

02/Feb/2021 03:12 PM

You can always find a reason to justify what you're doing. But, that doesn't mean it makes what you're doing right.

*   *   *

02/Feb/2021 08:27 AM

How much time must pass before your sins should be forgotten?

When you are asleep and having a dream, what participation do you have in that dream? Most likely, you are in the middle of the happenings. Maybe you are to one side witnessing what is happening to someone else. But, you are there. You are interactive with the central action of that play.

Though most will conclude that dreams are nothing more than something that is happening in the mind of one specific individual, they are nonetheless an ideal example of human reality—of your reality. You are there, you are living, you are acting out, you are witnessing the doings of others, you are a participant. If you were not there, you would have no idea about what was taking place.

Your life is very much like this. The living of your life is very much like this. Your life is based upon your participation in any life situation and only you know what is truly going on because you are the one living it.

Think about your life. Think about the things you have lived. Think about what you are living now. Who is living it? The answer: you are living it. All of your reality is based upon what you are doing.

Think about any life situation you have lived. It was you who lived it. Maybe you loved what was going on, maybe someone was making you very happy, maybe you hated what was going on, maybe someone really pissed you off, but you were at the center of it. It was you living that moment. Maybe you were somewhere where you were totally board. But, who was feeling that? You.

Sometimes we witness the life interactions of others. Sometime we watch something that makes us happy, makes us sad, makes us laugh, or makes us cry. Mostly, we watch a whole lot of life go by. We watch people passing us by all the time: talking, driving, walking, and doing what they do. Though we have no involvement in their life actions, nonetheless, it is we who are witnessing it. Thus, it all makes up the life experience of our lives.

Have you ever had someone describe a life story that you lived? Maybe they even lived it with you but when they tell the story something is missing, something is not quite right. Why is that? Because it is not you telling the story. Their life assessment and terms of experience are different from your. Even if they were there, even if they lived that moment with you, their definition of that experience is based upon their own conception of reality. Each person's definition of reality is always, at least partially, different from someone/anyone else's.

So, what does all this tell us? It tells us that you must embrace your reality, you must live your life, you must experience your life to the best of your ability; no matter if your love or if you hate what is going on. Why? Because the experiencing of your life is all you have. It is only you truly experiencing it. If you space out, if you tune out, if your turn off, all that you have lived is lost because you are the only one who is truly living your life.

Pretty much everybody has the dream of becoming whatever it is they hope to become. Some take steps towards actualizing that dream. Many, however, do not.

Though most people have the dream of BECOMING, the steps you take to get there highly define your ability to reach that end goal. Think about it, what are you doing today to help you become what you hope to become?

The fact of life is, the facts of life take over many a life. This is one of the main reason people are kept from accomplishing all they hope to achieve.

Some people are luckily; they come from financially secure, supportive families. These families are open to helping their family members in becoming all that they hope to be. Many people are not that luckily, however. They must fend for themselves from a young age. They must get a job to pay their bills: to eat and to keep a roof over their head.

Here's where things get complicated. The job you choose to do is going to be instrumental it either helping you or hindering you from achieving all that you hope to become. Sure, sure, there are those people who rise to the top of any game who did some pretty unsavory things as a way to make a living in their route to the top. But, those people are the exception, they are not the rule. Most people who enter into a less that dream-helpful type of employment are cast to dwell within that realm forever.

There is the tale that is very prominent here in Hollywood, and that is well known all across the globe, about the person who is a food server: a waiter or a waitress, but what they truly believe they will become is a famous actor. As a filmmaker, I have met so many people who are making their living doing this job who believe they will ascend to the top of the acting game. They are taking acting classes, they have their professional headshot which they send out to casting calls, they are doing all of the things that they believe will pay off but what they are not doing is acting in front of the camera. Each day, they go to work, but their work is not causing them to rise up in their chosen game. Years later, in some cases decades later, I have re-met a person and they are still hoping to act but what they are really doing is being a food server. That has become the definition and the reality of their life.

That is just one example but it is a very clear expression of how what you do becomes what you are. It also shows how what you do either adds to or takes away from what you will ultimately become.

People make all kinds of excuses for why they do what they do. It is important to note, however, that in many cases these excuses become the definition of their life. I cannot tell you how many times, throughout my life, that I have encountered someone telling me about all they were going to become and all they were going to achieve but at the end of the day all they ever became was the job they were doing.

So, what does this tell us about life and what does this tell us about how what you do to pay your bills can either help you in becoming what you desire to be or hinder you?

Take a look at your own life… What are you truly doing to become all that you hope to be? What did you do yesterday? What are you doing today? What will you do tomorrow? Is the job you are doing to pay your bills actually a pathway to your life-dream of achievement? Or, is it just something you do? Maybe you love it, maybe you hate it but what does it do in helping you achieve your end goal?

If you truly hope to become something it is essential that you truly take a look at what you are doing to get there. You really need to analyze how all of the things that you do during each day of you're life affect the overall evolution of your life.

For all of us who are adults, for all of us who are an independent person, we must find a way to make a living. But, be careful what you choose to do to make that living, as it may become all you will ever become.

Standing Up For Your Rights
While You Kill Other People
29/Jan/2021 12:49 PM

It's a rainy day in L.A. today. I had to head over to my local Guitar Center to return a guitar I ordered from them on-line as they had sent me the wrong model. I got there at 10:00 AM, the time that is stated on their website that they open, but they were still closed. A sign on the door read, due to COVID we now open at 11:00AM. Though I was bit annoyed, I took the time to go and check out a local thrift store in the area, very aware of the fact that I had a very expensive guitar sitting on the front seat of my car. Anyway, I got back to GC at 11:00 and the return was painless.

En route home, I stopped at my local supermarket to pick up dinner. As it was raining, and I didn't have a raincoat with me, I walked quickly towards the door. Just as I got to the door I realized I didn't have my mask on. I quickly put it in place. Walking in just behind me was a guy wearing a hoody. He didn't have his mask on either. I jestingly stated, *"You forgot your mask."* He thought I was joking but then he felt his face, *"What happened to it?"* He turned around to go and figure out the whereabouts of his mask.

FYI, right now we are in the time of the COVID-19 coronavirus pandemic. New strains have entered the U.S and the number of cases are surging. As such, and because of, masks are required in all stores and places like that.

Anyway, inside the store, I grabbed what I came for. As I was walking over towards the dairy section, I noticed a couple that wasn't wearing masks. They were a very normal looking couple:

Caucasian, maybe early forties. My first thought was, maybe they forgot theirs like I or the guy behind me at the door had done. As all of the other people in the store were avoiding them like they had the plague (maybe they do), I smiled, underneath my mask of course, and stated, *"You've not wearing your mask." "Good observation,"* they guy snidely replied. This made me laugh. They were obviously, Trumpians. That's the term I affectionately use to refer to the Anti-Maskers, COVID's a hoaxer, Anti-Vaxers, and the Stop the Steal people.

Now, we all have our opinions about this COVID-19 situation. I know I do. We all have opinions about the way the government has handled this crisis. I know I do. But, the fact of the fact is, people are dying. A lot of people have died. Even more have gotten very sick and were hospitalized; including some members of my extended family. And, no matter how much you wish to exercise your rights of liberty, (defined by whatever country you live in), you have the potential to be a killer and not even know it.

Yes, there are now a few vaccines released worldwide. But, I can't get one yet. Can you? Distribution is a mess. And, though there are vaccines, people are still getting sick and dying because so few people have been vaccinated.

So, there they were, this arrogant couple, not caring of the potential they had to kill any person they came into contact with. Do you think that's right?

When I was at the self-checkout, check stand, I heard the notice go out over the loudspeakers, detailing that for the safety of everyone all people in the store must wear masks. It's a business; they have the right to set their own rules. And, in this time in the history of humanity, wearing a mask is not a bad idea. I don't like to wear one either but I care more about the greater good of society than simply what I believe and what I feel like.

I'm sure the manager went up and talked to them and ask them to put on a mask or leave. Maybe there was a confrontation. Maybe it will be on YouTube or the News, I don't know? Maybe that's what that couple wanted. It seems a lot of people are looking to become famous by any means possible. Again, I don't know? But, what I do know is, now, you have the potential to kill someone if you are infected with this disease. You may have it and not even know it. So, you could kill someone and not even know that it was you that caused them to die. But, does that make you any less of a killer?

There is a part of me that believes people who behave in that non-caring fashion should be the one's who get and suffer from the disease, they should be the one's who lose loved ones. But, that is just not necessarily in the cards. Sometimes the arrogant get away with murder. But, right is right. Caring is caring. If you can't even care enough about your fellow human beings to wear a mask when you are in public that, in and of itself, defines entirely the type of person that you are: selfish and ignorant.

The Out of Body Experience

In some circles of the vast plethora of advancing spirituality, there is a certain subset of practitioners that advocates achieving the out of body experience. But, what exactly is that: what does it mean, what does it prove, and what does it provide the zealot?

The out of body experience is achieved via various means. Certainly, for anyone who has ever taken hallucinogens, the out of body experience is quite common. The sensation and experience where your consciousness has become removed from your body and you can actually look down at your physical form and observe what you are doing is a common experience.

This sensation is not limited to a drug induced experience, however. Many people, when they are close to death, are said to have this experience. Though I have been close to death a couple of time in my life, I did not experience that but, as a young child, for better, for worse, or otherwise, I used to possess the ability to create that experience at will. But, what did it prove? What does that experience prove? From my assessment, nothing of true importance to the overall spiritual grow or evolvement of the individual.

There are some schools of spiritual thought that teach what has come to be called, Astral Projection. In brief, that is the ability to transport your consciousness to other places or ethereal realms in order to communicate with entities that exist in other worlds. The problem with this entire concept is that it is un-provable. At best, it is simply someone claiming that they can transcend the boundaries of this reality and move into another. But, where is the proof? Where is the documentation? Where is the standard of verification of this practice? It is simply them saying that they are doing something and/or communicating with some entity in some other undefined realm. It is not like two people speaking on a telephone. Therefore, there is no proof. And, just like all of those so-called psychics out there who practice certain techniques where they develop the ability to guide the patterns of thought and manipulate the minds of the people who wish to believe in order to make them trust in what they have to say in order to gain whatever it is they hope to gain: money, power, fame, or control, it is all an undefined illusion.

On the other side of the issue, the fact is, there are some people who are a little tilted. There are some who believe the lie they are telling themselves. Their mental perspective is a bit off and they allow their own mind to drift into the spectrum of false reality. Though they may believe what they are feeling, and even what they are saying to others in regards to their mental experiences, it must be noted, it is only their mental experience; not yours. Thus, as it is not the common experience, what they are claiming is only experienced in their own mind. Is that real? Is that true reality? Or, is that simply insanity?

When you look to the vast amount of literature that has been created over the years about transcending the body and mentally moving to some other realm, every technique is different. If this practice were true, wouldn't there be one pathway? Wouldn't that be the only method that was discussed? Moreover, if this out of body experience actually provided a solid benefit, wouldn't it by now be proven to be a reality and wouldn't it be taught as a ratified higher religious practice? But, it is not.

Throughout time, people, particularly those who walk on the so-called spiritual path, wish to exhibit their advanced knowledge and present themselves as possessing something someone else does not understand. The claimed ability to leave their body is an ideal example of this as it is so unprovable. Thus, it simply becomes a means for the claimant to proclaim that they can do something that you cannot. Maybe these people even make a few bucks by lecturing or writing a book on the subject. Certainly, their ego is stroked. As for everyone else; the believers, they are left in awh of what that person claims that they can do. Maybe they even give them money to communicate with that abstract supposed something that lurks out there in the realms of the unknown. But, what does all of this equal? Nothing. It does not change reality. It does not change the truth of reality. It does not change the reality of reality. It simply becomes another mind game designed by one person to pretend to be something more than the other person and a reason for the gullible to believe.

The truth of life is, reality is reality. It is a simply as that. People live; people die, and people try to find something to fill their time in-between birth and death.

You can spend your time trying to transverse into some undefined realm if you want to but what does that actually give to your life? What will it do for the betterment of all human kind? You can believe in the claims made by the aberrant mystics if you want to, but how do you know what they are saying is true?

If you want to find a higher human consciousness, if you want to be the best vehicle for spirituality that you can be; BE it is a simply as that. BE as pure, BE as honest, BE as locked into true reality as you can BE. BE, for this reality is all we truly have. Everything else is simply a promised illusion.

The Things That No Longer Matter
28/Jan/2021 09:18 AM

For each of, as we pass through life, there comes to be things that define who and what we were. ...Things that we remember fondly and things that hold a place in our heart.

For each person, these things are different. What one person may hold close to their heart another person may find to be quite ridiculous.

For some, these items are childhood toys. For others they may be a bicycle, a motorcycle, or a car. For me, it's things like guitars, 4-Track reel-to-reels, 4-Track cassette decks, and cameras like the Sony VX2000, (the greatest indie production camera ever).

The thing is, technology changes so these items have fallen by the wayside, at least in terms of functionality. For some of these items, they have become quite collectable and their price is very high. In some cases, more than what they actually cost new. But, that does not provide them with the functionality they once held.

For some, who have lived a very stable lifestyle, they were allowed to keep the original items that they once owned throughout their life. That's great! For others, like myself, who was moved around a lot as a kid and never really had a home, even to this day, things come and go. When they are gone, they are missed, and there is always a whole left where they once existed.

The thing about life is, time deteriorates. Nothing lasts forever. So, no matter how much you take care of an item, that item is not destiny to live throughout eternity. Though certainly, some items have more longevity than others.

175

So, what does this leave us with? What does this leave us with as we all hold the same feelings—the memory and the love for that something we once owned? It leaves us with the reality of life. It defines for us the realism of the experience of life. We have, we had, we want again. But, what we had then, we can never truly have now, because all we truly have is our experience in this moment, not that moment. And, though we hope and try to relive what we felt then, this now is not that then. It is now, it is who we are now; it is not what we were then.

So, though we all look back with fond memories to what we had then and how it made us feel—and though in some cases we can repurchase that once owned item, we have to chalk all of this up to the reality of reality. This moment is not that moment and if we are locked into a time gone past, we can never truly experience the perfection of what we are living now.

You Can Always Tell the People
Who Are Destined for Greatness
26/Jan/2021 02:18 PM

Pretty much everyone hopes to do something great with their life. They hope to do that something or be that something that will propel them to living a grand life and to be well-respected and well-remembered while possibly giving to others and the greater world as a whole. But, the fact of the matter is, very few people will ever reach that level of achievement. There are an untold number of reasons for this: some are where and how a person was born and raised, others are more personal; based on how they behave and the things that they choose to do. But, the reality of reality is, few people every reach any level of greatness in their life.

This being said, you can immediately tell a person who is bound for greatness. They have a demeanor, they possess a mindset, they are directed, and they act and do all things Life in a very specific manner.

There have been tons of books written on the subject of how to, *"Become."* Motivational speakers talk all the time attempting to guide people towards their own greatness. But, no matter how many word are written or spoken it is the individual who either is or is not bound to do something great.

Just as a person who is bound for greatness can be observed, the individual who is compelled towards just the opposite can be spotted. They are the people who are confrontational, those who lie, deceive, cheat, steal, treat other people badly, believe they are better than others, are judgmental, are confrontational, are egotistical, lie to themselves

177

about why they do what they do, and the list goes on and on. We all know the type. Some of these people even hide behind their belief that the reason they behavior in a non-productive, hurtful manner is in order to do for others. But, by scolding, by judging, by chastising, by attacking, by hurting, by lying for whatever reason may be in their mind, all they have done is to damage the Life Space of someone else, and by casting their own judgment onto any life situation all they have illustrated is that they are simply a person locked into a space of their own knowingness and righteousness. Behaving in this manner only demeans others. And, from doing any of this, nothing good is ever born.

Some people believe that they will be Great. In fact, some people tell others that this will be their destiny. This is especially the case when a person is young before the realities of existence have set in. But, for anyone who broadcasts this, it is almost an assured sign of what they are not to become.

So, is there a pathway to greatness? The simply is yes. It is tread only by those who stay in the realm of goodness. ...Those who walking hand-in-hand with nature. Those who do not deny their placement in life and/or do not try to overturn the obvious decisions of god. Those who continually and only say and do good things.

The broader answer to the question is that, it is very complicated. There is no direct pathway to greatness no matter how much good you do and how much happiness you bring to others. But intended purpose, that is the key. Those destine for greatness follow a predetermined path of self-knowing, self-acceptance, and being true to themselves while embracing their own wholeness, hand-in-hand with bringing betterment to the life of all those they encounter.

So… Everybody wants to be great. Though few will achieve this, the best thing you can do is to do the things that those who are considered to be great have proven is the right pathway. Be good. Be kind, Be truthful. Be helpful. Consciously never hurt anyone. Say good things. Do good thing. Help everyone you can. Then, even if you never come to be considered as GREAT, at least you will be remembered by the people you encountered with found memories. And, that is a definition of greatness in and of itself.

*   *   *

If you define yourself by what someone says you are, then all you can ever be is what someone else has decided that you have become.

The Liars Have All the Answers
25/Jan/2021 10:37 AM

Way back in the way back when I had met this girl. We met via my involvement with Swami Satchidananda and the Integral Yoga Institute. She had come to take a class. Me, I was young, and veering away from the Bramacharya mindset. Her, she was pretty. We began to hang out which all turned out to be a big mistake but that is an entirely different story.

At the time, I was living in the Valley and going to college. She was living down in the O.C.

Like many people of the era, she was seeking spiritual understanding. Also, like many people of the era, she moved between teachers attempting to find the path that best suited her.

One night, she invited me to visit this one teacher she had been working with. He was a Caucasian guy who operated a yoga studio out of an upstairs unit in what may best be described as a strip mall. I believe, forty years or so later, he is still there.

Anyway, he went by this holy sounding Sanskrit name. When I entered the room and sat down he came up to me, as he could see I was new, to introduce himself. He asked about me and I told him I was a student of Swami Satchidananda. I could immediately tell this struck him as disconcerting as he now had someone within his ranks who must know his stuff. All the others were just those people seeking a route to the promised enlightenment of the era or a father figure. Both of these were a very gullible type. When I told him what I told him, he began to laugh and laugh and laugh. It was so contrived. I could immediately see this was one of those ploys to throw someone off their game. But, I have always been the wrong person to play mind games with, even back when I was young.

The evening went on. The man gave his lecture. We did the meditation session, etc... We left. I, of course, never returned.

There are so many people full of so much bullshit that it is almost hard to believe. They gather borrowed knowledge from this book, that lecture, that whatever, and then dish it out as if it is their own. Some, like this guy, added orange robes and a Sanskrit name to the equation, just to provide more apparent authenticity. But, all of that never changes the bullshit.

I have encountered a lot of people like that throughout the years. Certainly, far more back in the 1970s than today but truly little has changed. And, that is the problem with seeking. The people who seek want to be given something—they want to be provided with that some imagined something. But, due to the illusive nature of that abstract something what they are given can never be proven or disproven. That/this is why so many people fall prey to the manipulative words and hands of the liar.

A couple of years later, I think I was twenty-one. I was at the Bodhi Tree Bookstore one day, which was then the mecca for spiritual knowledge in L.A., and I noticed that this Eastern Yogi was going to give a lecture. I had always enjoyed listening to what different teachers had to say, so I decided to go. When I got there, I found that the lecture was to be given in this very rundown section of Hollywood, in this old street front business. Whatever... I went inside and there were like three people in attendance. The guy walked in. He was a true Eastern Yogi. Even though there were only a few people there, he gave his talk. It was completely uninspired. Nonetheless, after the lecture, I went up to meet him. Nice guy. A true believer/a true liver. What was the difference between this man and the aforementioned individual? Heritage and purpose. He wasn't making excuses for doing the things that a true yogi should not be doing, whereas the other man was. One was in it as a business; the other was in it as a life and a lifestyle.

So, here's the thing... You can claim to be something. You can read and study all of the books on the subject. You can even change your name to something grand and auspicious, and maybe even get a diploma or a proclamation, but you cannot change the essence of your being—you cannot change who and what you truly are. Whenever you go to any teacher, you really need to remember that. Are they doing what they are doing as a business? Or, are they giving what they know to you for free? If they're a business, then they're a businessperson. If they are true to whom they are and what they have to teach, then they will give it to you for free.

The problem is, the world is full of liars. Most teachers are liars. This is especially the case when they are not at an accredited institution like a place of higher education. These people can say whatever they want. They can claim whatever they want. They tell each person what they think they want to hear in order to get their money, their body, their loyal, their whatever... But, at the root of all truth, at the heart of each true teacher, is the person who is truly themselves—the person who has no need to lie or develop students or clientele. If a teacher is looking to get more students then they are lost in the mindset of conquest. How can any individual who is on a quest to get more of something or someone in their life be a true person—how can they be trusted? If a person seeks nothing and gaining no one more, then why would they need to claim to be anything? Why would they need to lie?

The truth of a person is self-evident. How do you know a person is a true person that can be trust? They claim nothing.

Remember, the liars have all the answers. If someone is telling you what you want to hear, if someone is promising you anything, be very weary of that person because they are obviously hoping to gain something for themselves.

*   *   *

Are you aware of the fact of what you did and who you did it to?

How does that make you feel?

I was having lunch with a friend of mine when an interesting situation occurred. But, before I get into all of that let me give you a little bit of the backstory.

I am writing this during the time of the COVID-19 coronavirus pandemic. At least here in California, the restaurants have all been ordered to close. They are not allowed to offer indoor dining. During this time period they are only allowed to offer take-out. One of the ways some restaurants have been getting around this is that, previously they were allowed to offer outdoor dining. From this, many restaurants set up, in some cases, elaborate parking lot tent facilities and/or in some cities they have actually taken away the street parking allowing restaurants to set up their tables and their chairs in the streets; bounded by makeshift walls, of course. Though they are not currently supposed to do this, in order to keep business coming in, some restaurants have put their tables back up and allowed patrons to sit at them as long as they buy their food to-go.

With all that out of the way, back to the storyline…

Anyway, my friend and I had picked up some food and we were on our way back to her place to eat it. As we walked past, there were two aging Korean men sitting at one of those tables that aren't really supposed to be used. They both had coffees in to-go cups and one of them was even smoking which is totally verboden in association with all California dining establishments. But, you know how Korean men can be... (Maybe you don't?)

Anyway... The one guy was wiping down his phone with one of those single use packaged wipe things that look kind of like a Handi Wipe. He had a couple more of the packets lying on the table. As we walked by my friend surprisingly asked the guy, *"Can I have one of those?"* He looked at her. He looked at me. He looked at his friend. He said something under his breath to his friend in Korean. And, then he handed her one. *"Thank you,"* my friend exclaimed in all of her youthful exuberance. I observed as the two men both watched her walk away with her long legs extending below her short skirt. You know the kind of look I'm taking about.

She grabbed my hand and we were back on our way. She was happy, she got one of those whip things as she felt her phone needed it. I smiled and I explained to her, *"Now, you own that man everything."*

The thing about life is, and a thing that very few people ever contemplate is, that whenever you take something from someone, (given willingly or not), you owe that person. If you take something from them without their freewill of giving, forget about it, you really owe them. But, in life, most people simply want what they want and, small or large, as long as they get it, all is well with their world. But, they never think about the, (for lack of a better term), karma that is invoked by the act of taking.

Think about your taking... Think about how you feel when you get. It probably feels pretty good; right? You have gotten what you want.

Now, think about the act of giving. Giving may also feel good or it may feel bad. But, whatever the case, when you give, that personally costs you something. If you give something that means you had to get something. In most cases, getting means you had to earn the money to buy it. What did that earning cost your life? How much time did it take? How much work did it take? What did it do to your life?

Giving, whether it is in the form of something physical or something mental, first requires the getting. The getting always cost the giver something. This getting is never free. And, if you get, you owe the giver.

Again, most people never think about this. They just want. They just ask. They just take. They dismiss what that giving cost the giver because they are now content in what they have received.

If you wish to live a conscious life, you really need to be careful of your taking. For taking always sets the need of owing into motion. No matter how willingly anything is given to you, if you take you own that giver something. Maybe, you owe them everything.

Depending on how the term is intended to be used, the most common Sanskrit words utilized to express the concept of destiny are, *"Daiva,"* or, *"Adrishta."*

Destiny is this strange undefined thing that people put into play when something either happens to their life in a positive or a negative manner. *"That was just your destiny…"* Or, *"This is my was destiny…"* But, what is destiny and what does it truly mean?

For each of, we seek to find a definition to the happenings in our life and the lives of others. We seek someone or something to blame. When good things happen, some but not all of us, give thanks. But, who is that thanks given to? …Some mystical, undefined, Out There being. When negative things occur, we seek someone to blame. But, who is to blame? Is it that same mystical, undefined, Out There being or is it simply ourselves for placing ourselves where a specific type of events may happen to us?

Rarely, do people take full responsibility for the happenings in their life. They prefer to claim, *"It was a gift from god,"* or, *"Destiny sent me down this road."* But, what does any of this actually mean? What is destiny and why do people relinquish control of their life over to such an abstract concept?

We all understand what destiny is intended to mean. It is that something that was meant to happen to us that we have little or no control over. But, think about your life… What don't you have control over? Sure, you can decide to walk a path of goodness or you can decide to walk a path of badness. You can choose to help or you can choose to hurt. You can choose to go to the left or you can choose to go to the right. You can choose to associate with a certain person or a specific type of people, but is any of that destiny? No, that is simply what you choose to do based upon the choices you are allowed to make.

People lie to themselves all the time about the happenings in their life. They give thanks or they blame others. Why do most people do this? They do this either because they don't want to take personal responsibility for their actions or they have been programmed into feeling that they are not worthy of holding control over their own life. But, you are in control! What you do is what you choose to do. What happened to you is not destiny it is simply a reaction to your action of making a choice.

Where you place yourself in life comes to define what happens to your life. What you choose to do in each situation that occurs in your life, defined by where you have chosen to place yourself in your life, is what occurred by where you choose to be and what you choose to do.

Destiny is an excuse. Take responsibility for your own choices.

You Are A Worker Bee
21/Jan/2021 12:45 PM

For all of us... At least all of us who are adults... We must find a way to make a living. ...A way to make our way through this world. We must pay our bills and pay for a place to live. For many of us, that means we must get a job. For some, that job is simply a way to make a living. ...A way to make enough money to live life. For others, their job is their life. All that they do revolves around their job.

I think to my father. He was all in at his job. So much so, that he literally had a heart attack and died while at his job. My mother, she was all about her job, as well. She was a woman who did not drive, yet she took the bus to work each day: rain or shine. When she was finally forced into retirement, due to her age, she had nothing to do as she had never developed any outside interests. Bored and with no purpose, she passed on a year or so later.

Most people are worker bees. They do not develop their own business. They never know what true responsibility is. They prefer to work for others so they can just collect a paycheck at the end of the week. Life is much easier that way. Then, they always have someone to complain about and blame. If they do something wrong, they may get scolded, at worst they may get fired, but it is not their business that will come crashing down. So, they are free from any true responsibility.

Some people, some of the worker bees, they get all involved with their job. They let it go to their head. They let it become their empowerment. They let it drive their ego. They allow it to become a vehicle for them to express their opinions about life and other people. I call people like this a, *"Mouthy Maven."* They speak, maybe they yell, maybe they are rude, maybe they even attack others, but all they are is a worker bee. They exist via a position of service that they were given by someone else. Yet, the Mouthy Mavens are not providing the customer with a service at all. They step beyond their job description. As a consumer, these are the people you sometimes have to deal with; the one's who really ruin your shopping (or whatever) experience. Yet, there they are getting paid.

In times gone past, in life, in places like India, there was a very detailed Cast System, where people were told what they could become. In most of life, it is really not that different. We are all defined by who we were born to, what was the level of their life, and if we become educated, earn the right degrees, and progress to the highest level we can based upon the amount of support or financial aid we are provided with. But still, much of our progress is defined by where we began.

Thus, we get back to the worker bees… The people who work to make society function. They are the core of societal existence.

Here's the thing… Unless you were born into a lot of money, and your family is willing to give it to you, you are probably going to be/become a worker bee. That's the law of averages. So, what are you going to do with this fact? How are you going to process this fact? Are you going to live your life defined entirely by your job? Are you going to use your job to provide you with a means to actually live life the way you had hoped? Or, are you going to become a Mouthy Maven and ruin the experience of others who come into contact with you while you are doing your job?

Everything you do while in the experience of your life is defined by what you choose to do within that experience. It is defined by how you choose to think? It is defined by how you choose to analyze that experience. It is defined by how you allow that experience to cause you to act. At the root sourcepoint of your life is YOU. But, if you must deal with others while you do what you do, then at that moment karma is set into play. How you behave towards others while in that/any situation is going to define the next set of options in your life and what you will encounter next and next and next in your life. So, if you are a worker bee, what are you going to create within that experience of your job? What are you going to allow it to do for your life? What are you going to allow it to do to the life of other people?

As in all cases, what you do, how you choose to behave, and how you interact with others, comes to be the definition of your life. What is the definition of your life? What will be the definition of your life? How will what you do to earn a living to survive define the all and the everything of what becomes of your life? If you do not contemplate these things, you will never truly understand your life, yourself, or how you have arrived at where you have arrived.

Thanks for Mentioning Me in Your Book

21/Jan/2021 09:20 AM

"In Samurai Vampire Bikers From Hell (1992), renowned actor and martial artist Scott Shaw tried to combine motorcycles and martial arts. Shaw acted here as director and lead actor. In this film, his character drives his Harley-Davidson to Hollywood to rid the city of ancient vampires with his companion."

This is the is translation of an excerpt from a book titled, Два колеса в зеркале экрана. This title translates, (via Goggle Translate), as, Two Wheels in the Mirror of the Screen. As I don't speak (or read) Russian, I don't know if that is a good translation of the title or not but that's alls I's gots… Overall, it seems to be an interesting book composed about biker films.

I've always been intrigued by Russian heritage and culture. There's just something majestic about the architecture and their history. Never been there. Always seemed a little too totalitarian for me. Maybe someday… Nonetheless, one of my films and I are mentioned in a book published in Russia.

Being mentioned in the writings of other people always kind of strikes me in a strange way. Having my films mentioned in books is also kind of weird. But, I guess it does all go to the point and principle of creation: you create, other people see what you have created, and it causes them to think and possible write about it. That's a good thing right?

Most people, when they write (or speak) about my films simply want to critique them—put their own seal of approval or disapproval upon them and maybe detail what they believe must have been the creative or production process that was involved in their creation. Though in most cases they are generally wrong in their assessment, but that's okay, I guess... At least they're thinking about my films.

But, this all goes to the definition and evolution of culture. You know, recently I was watching this documentary called, The Booksellers, on Amazon Prime. As the title implies, it's about booksellers and book collectors, particularly in the New York market. It's a pretty good doc.

One of the points they brought up in it, via one of the interviewees, is how books are out there forever, where as there are so many magazines, magazine articles, and magazine authors that have become lost in the changing of time. Me, I remember when there were millions of magazines on the newsstand. I used to love to go to this one newsstand in Hollywood at one or two in the morning and simply explore and take in all this knowledge. But, that era is gone, as are most of the magazines.

The thing is, once those magazines are gone they are gone. They were not assembled like books to last for a long-long period of time. Most people just threw them away when they were done with them. I know that there are a few magazine that my poetry was published in or my films or I were mentioned in that I have been searching for years to acquire. Searching, with no luck.

This one person in the doc was drawn to magazine collecting via hip-hop culture and her desire to explore the times gone past. Thus, that is the focus of her collection. That's great. Archiving history is very-very important. But, most people don't do that. Most people don't read books. Most people don't care. Now/today, at best, people read a few lines on the intent and that is the extent of their research. But, with that, so much is lost.

Books, in many cases, find their way to being digitized. The writing is cast to eternity. But, things like magazines, so few ever have been digitized, so few ever will be. From this, lost will be the creations, the research, and the writing art of the authors forever. Not good.

Life, time, history, people, it all evolves, it all/always changes. Pretty much everything was the same for eons but now change is in hyper drive. But, with this rapid change so much truth, so much literature, so much journalism, and so much written art is lost.

Remember to read. Remember to archive. Remember to collect. And, if you are a writer, thanks for mentioning me!

The Realness of What You Are

Every now and then I am contacted about the legacy of my friend Kris Derrig and the Les Paul's that he created. In brief, back in the 1980s, Kris produced electric guitars in the exact style of the late 1950s Gibson Les Paul's. There's an article on this website if you wish to read a little deeper into the subject. He worked out of my friend Jim Foote's Music Works, then located in Redondo Beach, California. During this era, a lot of rock star bands of the time rehearsed at Jim's rehearsal studio behind the shop. One of the bands that was there was Guns n' Roses prior to their rise to superstardom. Their manager saw one of Kris' guitars and bought it for Slash who used it on some of the recordings on their debut album, Appetite for Destruction. Thus, the Kris Derrig Les Paul was set to infamy. Sadly, Kris passed away at the very young age of thirty-two in 1987 from lung cancer, most probably due to sucking in all the glues and the paint flumes of guitar production, as he never wore a mask, before the establishment of his fame was ever solidified.

Many people now seek out the very few Kris Derrig Les Paul's that were created. In fact, some people even claim that they have one when they do not. There has become an entire cult surrounding these guitars.

As stated, I am sometimes contacted by someone wondering if what they have is a true Kris Derrig and/or if I know where they can buy one. They have become very-very valuable.

One of the things I remind people of, when they are contemplating buying one his guitars is that, though it is a good guitar, the only reason anybody knows about Kris or his Les Paul's is because Slash played one for a time. Though that is certainly not the only guitar Slash has ever played or recorded with. And, if it were not for this fact, no one would even know who Kris was. His guitars would just be Gibson replicas as were and are still created by other advanced luthiers.

But, all of this sends us to the question, what is real? No, his guitars were not Gibson's as stated on their headstocks. But yet, they have become much more valuable that true Gibson's made in that same era. Is the only reason they are valuable because people like Slash, Lenny Kravitz, and Charlie Daniels played one? Thus, are they only valuable due to what people perceive them to be? But, the fact is, even if you own one, it is not going to transform you into Slash. You are not (necessary) going to record a seminal album like, Appetite for Destruction. And remember, that was not the only guitar Slash used while recording that album.

So, what does this leave us with? Answer: It leaves us with perception. A person's perception of what is or is not real and/or what is or is not valuable; based solely upon what one is instructed to believe.

What do you believe is valuable? And, why do you believe it? Mostly, who told you to believe it?

What is real and what is fake? And, what sets the difference between their value?

Moreover, who are you? Are you truly what you are? Or, are you a fake hiding in your skin with the label and logo of something you are not?

Life is a strange conglomeration of presentations, acceptances, and beliefs. Just like the

Kris Derrig Les Paul, many times what you see is not what it truly is but does that/should that assign a value to the perception of that thing or that person?

In life, it is always proclaimed that the best person is the person who does not lie or deceive people about who or what they truly are. How about you? How true are you to true? And, do you lie about who or what you truly are? Do you lie about who are what you truly are even to yourself?

You really need to think about these things as you walk through your life because truth or fake truly can come to define your entire life.

In closing, Kris was a close friend. It was so sad to see him leave this world. His girlfriend from high school, who he was in a band with, contacted me several years ago thanking me for the page I have on this site devoted to him. A lot of people did and still do care about him. He was really a good guy. This world is far less because of his passing.

16/Jan/2021 02:43 PM

Remember: Your interpretation of a person is never a true definition of who that individual is or was.

The Black Belt and What it Means Today

For those people are not directly involved with the martial arts, when they hear someone has a black belt, they immediately assume that person possesses some advance and cunning skill of potentially deadly self-defense. For the person who is involved with the martial arts, when they think of the black belt, they see it as a goal but from there the degrees of that black belt, and the stripes on that black belt, must go up exponentially if they hope to compete in a world of the massive amount of so-called advanced black belts that exist in the world today.

During the late 1960s and early 1970s, via people like Chuck Norris and Bruce Lee, it became quite acceptable for people to study and train in varying forms of the fighting arts. Though this certainly moved the evolution of the martial arts along rapidly, there also came to be a problem with this method of intermingling. Previously, up to this point in time, a person studied one form of the martial arts from one instructor or within one organization. From this, an individual's actual understanding and necessary advancement within the art could be correctly assessed. When an individual was ready to earn a black belt, they were tested and upon passing that test were awarded that belt. When they were ready to move up another dan, (degree), after additional years of training, they were tested and if they passed that test they were promoted. It was all done via a very defined and pronounced method. What happened with the modern intermingling of the arts was, however, that defined ability became lost to eclecticism. Thus, what was once an expected definition of technique and/or ability became muddled.

Certainly, when the martial arts became widely accepted and taught in the West, traditions began to be lost. As the western mindset commonly focuses on self-advancement, business ownership, and self-adoration, numerous schools, new styles of the martial arts, and organization were given birth to. In many cases, these groupings lost contact with their Asian origins. From this, again, tradition was lost.

I am often reminded of a conversation I had with pioneering western martial artist, Bill, *"Superfoot,"* Wallace, when I was asked to write an article about him for a magazine. He profoundly stated, *"Back in the day if a person was a 1st degree black belt they were impossible to touch. If they were a 2nd degree black belt, forget about it, they would tear you apart. Now, everyone is an 8th, 9th, or 10th degree black belt and they are terrible."* This fact has become a byproduct of the modernization of the martial arts, particularly in the western world, and why the entire definition of what truly is or is not a black belt has come to be less understood. As I often say, *"Change does not necessarily make something better, it just makes it different."*

I remember beginning in the 1960s, one could purchase black belt training courses in magazines. Upon the completion of this course one would be awarded a black belt diploma with no testing required. Certainly, an intermediate or advanced practitioner of the martial arts, with a lot of actually physical training under their belt, may learn from written and/or illustrated material but for the novice that is virtually impossible. And, to earn a black belt via this method is perplexingly unrealistic. Yet, how many people earned a black belt in this manner?

As the 1970s dawned, and more and more westerners became black belts, the need for advancing one's black belt dan ranking continued to rise. Again, initially via magazines, numerous organizations arose that offered various forms of un-tested promotions. All of the organizations looked and sounded official. The diplomas they issued were well printed, making the barer appear to be all that they claimed to be.

These traditions of intermixing the martial arts, defining new systems of the martial arts, and creating new organization to back up the credentials of practitioners has continued forward onto today. What has been created? From my perspective, an eclectic mess of people marketing themselves, their schools, and their systems to the masses but possessing little true relevance of authenticity.

Remember, a diploma does not make a person a black belt. In fact, diplomas declaring a person's martial art ranking are a relatively new chapter in the very long history of the martial arts. Who and what a person is on the inside and how they treat and interact with other people on both a physical and a humanitarian level is what defines a true black belt.

So, what does this leave us with and how should the black belt be viewed in this modern, (particularly western), world? The answer is not entirely clear. But, what must be understood is that someone claiming to be a black belt today no longer means that they are truly that advanced master of physical movement that the wearing of the black belt once defined. Moreover, as more and more of the modern martial arts have placed their focus on the kill-or-be-killed mixed martial arts orientated physical moments, it must be comprehended that just because someone has learned how to beat someone up does not mean that they possess the advance understanding of human movement that the true, traditional, martial arts provides the practitioner.

In closing, the true martial arts are about physical mastery and advanced mental awareness. They are not about ego. They are not about what degree black belt a person claims to hold. In fact, a person's black belt degree should never be the reason you do or do not study from them or define how you evaluate them as a human being. The holding of a black belt or the degree of the black belt a person claims can only be truly defined by who and what that person is and what they do for the greater good of the martial arts and society as a whole.

Judge any person by the goodness they say or do, not by whether or not they claim to be a black belt.

The true black belt gives without taking. They help without hurting. They give instead of receiving. They compliment instead of claiming.

15/Jan/2021 09:04 AM

What do you do when you're waiting?

What you do while your waiting defines who you are to become.

205

Ever since I was young, I would watch how some people who were in a position of power would dominantly extend that power over others. They knew that they had power, they knew what they could do with that power, thus, they would use their power to control the lives of others via various methods. Sometimes this control was demonstrated by physical means, sometimes it was verbal, but, whatever the case, these people, in a position of power, would use that power to dominate the life of others.

The thing about power is, however, power is fleeting. Yes, you may have it for a moment but if you use it to negative ends all that occurs is that you will be destroyed by your own use of that dominance. Not to mention that people will hold negative feelings about you which is a pathway to destruction in and of itself. This devastation may occur via various means, but power is only power as long as you are in control of that power. But, power, by its very nature, is transient—it does not last forever.

Certainly, we see people attempting to exhibit their power all the time. Maybe it is the boss at the job wanting their employees to get things done for them in a manner they find acceptable. Maybe it is a person in a relationship who wants to control their partner. Maybe it is the religious leader who believes that they know the only way people should morally behave. Certainly, it is the law enforcement professional or the politician who believes that they hold the power to make people act in the manner they deem acceptable. Maybe it is just the bully who is big or who knows how to fight and they exhibit their power over people via violence.

Speaking of which, I can tell a funny anecdote related to the school bully... When I was in kindergarten there was this one kid who felt he controlled the schoolyard. He would dominate via intimidation. Quite frequently he would come up to me and do that annoying thing, *"Look up, Look down, look at my finger,"* and then flick my nose. I told my father about what was going on and he said, *"The next time he does that why don't you punch him in the nose."* I later was told he was joking but that is exactly what I did. *"Look up, Look down,"* BAM I punched the kid right in the nose. He didn't fight back all he did was start crying while wiping the blood from his face. End of the bully... He never did that to me again.

People grow into power early in life. The more power they hold, the more power they are allowed to hold and the more power hungry they become. And, as we all know, some people do very negative things when they are in a position of power.

A lot of people strive their entire life to gain and then hold on to power. They do whatever it takes and they do not care who or what they hurt as long as they maintain that feeling of influence and supremacy.

Sometimes power comes in very strange forms. Sometimes people don't even see power as power but call it something else. But, the moment you hold influence over others you are in a position of power. If you find yourself in this life location you must be very careful for the essence of power cannot only overpower you and cause you to do bad things but it can hurt the life or one person or a lot of people. If you are intentionally seeking power, then you are already controlled by the lust for power. Thus, the negative aspects of this mindset control who and what you are and who or what you can become.

Power is dangerous. You must steer clear of people who use their power to control the lives of other. You must do this even is they do it with a smile on their face or by quoting the bible or the books of law.

What is the antidote to power? Kindness. Be kind. Whether you possess power or do not, always be kind and from this all life is allowed to be what it was meant to be.

Never seek power, as it is a false god that will eventually leave you destitute. Seek goodness. Seek caring. Seek helping. Seek kindness. Make the world a better place by possessing no power.

The Zen Filmmaking Tribe Just Got Smaller
13/Jan/2021 08:20 AM

Sadly, Julie Strain passed away a couple of days ago. She died from complication from dementia that she had been suffering from for the past several years. She believed she got dementia from a traumatic brain injury she incurred when she was in her early twenties from being thrown from a horse. Scary... Julie was four years younger than me and I too suffered a traumatic brain injury when I was in my early twenties when a car hit me while I was riding my motorcycle fracturing my skull in numerous places.

I always liked Julie. She was one of those very nice, very fun people. We spent a lot of time filming Zen Films at her home in Bel Air when she was married to Kevin Eastman. It was a great place. We used to call it the, *"Turtle Mansion,"* as Kevin is the co-creator to the *Teenage Mutant Ninja Turtles*. There was this gigantic painting of Julie that hung on the wall of the living room. I think that painting and its placement truly depicted who she truly was.

Julie was a talented person full of all kinds of fun and even crazy creative ideas. She was pretty much high all day long. She would get up, wake and bake, then smoke dope periodically all day long. I never smoked with her. I don't like the high, though she always offered. But, some of our cast and crew did partake from time to time. Then, come eight o'clock, she was off to bed. Had to get her beauty sleep.

Her house was always filled with the famous and the beautiful. The list of friends she had was astonishing. When I was there we would be sitting around with some of the A-list of Hollywood royalty or prominent porn stars.

During the time I was working with Julie she had a very high-end publicist. Via this pathway she invited Don and I to be on a couple of big TV shows she did. I remember this one time she was at an event called, *"Dragonfest,"* back in the late 90s. This was a martial arts meet and greet thing. I was invited, as obviously I've written a lot of stuff on the martial arts and have been involved forever but Julie and Kevin also had a signing table there that year. It was crazy, sure people knew about the *Ninja Turtles* and were waiting to get a signed photo of Kevin with the Turtles but most did not even know what Julie had or had not done but there was a mile long line to get her autographed photo. She was quite a presence. This, when just the year before, Kevin and I walked around the event and I had to tell people who he was. Kevin is also a great human being!!! I was always so thankful for what they both brought to our productions.

Julie was truly a one of a kind individual. With her passing, gone is one more piece of the puzzle to the original *Zen Filmmaking* troupe. First was Don, (Donald G. Jackson), then Karen (Black), Z'Dar, Conrad (Brooks), and now Julie. There is almost none of the original team left. Very sad! Julie was a great, beautiful (inside and out), talented individual and will truly be missed.

It's Easy to Say You Want To Do Something But It's Much Harder to Do It
10/Jan/2021 08:02 AM

How often do you think about doing something but do not do it? Maybe it is some creative project, maybe it is something that needs doing around your home, maybe it is reaching out to someone and doing something nice for them? How often you envision something in your mind and actually do it comes to be the definition of your life in the mind's eye of all of the people Out There. How often you envision something in your mind but do not do is comes to be the definition of all of things you could have been but were not.

Doing is the ultimate pathway of physical life. If you do, you do. If you don't, you don't. It is as simple as that.

Some people get motivated and do Some Thing hurtful. As I often speak of, anger is a powerful motivator. But, it is also a very negative one as this is the sourcepoint of so much hurt and damage in the world. Certainly, with the birth of the internet, this gave rise as a vehicle for many to vent their frustration at whatever or whomever. Keyboard Warriors abound. But, is that actually doing anything? It is doing but in this doing nothing positive is done. It is simply one person using their interpersonal dissatisfaction as a motivator to lash out. The person of consciousness never does this, however, as they understand that hurt or damage, based upon personal judgments, leads to nothing more than bad karma coming their own direction.

Doing with a conscious purpose is what True Doing is all about. This is where Good-ness is born.

So, let's get back to the question, *"How often do you think about doing something but do not do it?"*

When you envision something and do not actually do it do you truly study why you have not done it? Do you look inside yourself and find the reason why you did not do it?

For many, they will find a long list of excuses of why they can't or couldn't do it. For others, they simply write it off as that is just who they are. But, without the doing, nothing is done. Without the doing, you have accomplished nothing and have provided nothing positive or new to the greater whole of the world, life, humanity, and your own creative process.

So, take a moment. Right now, define what it is you would like to do creatively or otherwise. What can you do to do that something that you want to do and/or create? Do it! Set about on a path that will allow you today to bring that creation into reality.

The fact is, the more you do the more you are motivated to do. The more you actually do the more your mind is trained in the fact that it can be done.

So, what do you want to do? Do it. It will make you feel more whole and complete and it will be the gift of giving your creativity to the world.

Interestingly, President Trump was banned from Twitter today; apparently forever. They say it is due to his instigating the riot that took place at the Capital on Wednesday. Now, I'm not going to go into the who, what, when, where, or why about all that but what I am going to say is, think about it, the President of the United States of America, supposedly the most powerful person on the planet, has just been banned from using an internet platform by someone who does not like what he has to say. Wow!

From an unbiased perspective, that is pretty crazy when you think about it. A company, a person or persons at that company, are in control of the President of the United States of America. They are telling him what he can or cannot say or do on their platform. In times gone past, one would have thought that POTUS could do whatever he wanted. …That if some person or company would have messed with him throughout the centuries; look out. But, Twitter did it. They took away one of this man's favorite toys. It truly leaves me confounded.

But, the whole point to this little ditty is, if someone can do that to POTUS, if someone can control an individual in that massive position of power to that degree, why should you or I believe we have any power at all? I mean think about it, think about how many people are out there flexing their muscles, showing off their power everyday. Think how many tough guys (and girls) and how many bullies there are. Think about the people who flex their power in much more sublet ways. Most get away with it. They do so until someone bigger

213

and better steps up to them. But, for most of us, for the everyone else, we are simply trying to get by and live our lives as best we can. We do what we do, we like what we like, we dislike what we dislike, and maybe some of us even try to get our opinions out there. But, all that we say or do is ultimately controlled by that someone else.

The lesson is all this is, when you have no control you have no control. When you are not the person in the position of control you cannot take control. That person, that being, that entity, can take everything away from you and there is nothing that you can do about it. Scary, but true. Scary, but that is life.

So, what can we learn from all of this? Like I always say, *"You can only play in your own playground."* The moment you step outside of your safety zone, the moment you leave your space of control, you are out of control. The people or the powers-that-be can take things away from you, maybe things you really care about, and there is not a damn thing you can do about it.

That's why the truly transcendent person remains removed from all things World.

*   *   *

09/Jan/2021 07:03 AM

You can't remember what you don't remember.

Outer Self and the Project of the Inner Self
08/Jan/2021 09:43 AM

The moment you meet someone, they form an opinion about you. They do this by looking at what you are wearing, the way you wear your hair, what you say, and if they like the way you look or not. Within just a moment or two they decide who they believe you are and for many/for most they never change their opinion about you. Who they think you are is what they think you are and that is that. But, are you that person? Are you the person you project on the outside or are you something else?

For most of us, we wear the style of clothing that we feel best describes our life, our lifestyle, and our mindset. For most of us, we wear our hair in a manner that makes us feel good about ourselves. For most of us, we speak in the way we were taught to speak further defined by how we wish to be interpreted. But, think about the days that you wear something that you really do not like. Think about the time when you received that bad haircut. Think about the times when you spoke but the words just came out wrong. We have all been there. We have all experienced that. We have all met people during those periods of time. And, from this, people have drawn conclusions about us but where those conclusions correct?

Think about the people you have met as you have passed through your life. Maybe bring one or two of those people into clear focus—people that you actually remember your first meeting. What was you initial impression of them? Then, how much did your impression of them changed over the days, weeks, months, or years that you knew them?

216

Very little, I would imagine. Yes, you may have gotten to know them better, you may have become aware of some of the intricacies of their personality, (good or bad), but did your initial definition of them ever truly change? Probably not.

Most people live in a space of life presentation. They intentionally project to the world how they wish to be viewed. Who a person is becomes defined in their own mind. Within each culture, within each subculture, a person becomes who and what they can become and then they project that self-defined person to the world via clothing, hairstyle, and mostly words.

Think about the priest, what do they wear? They wear a style of clothing that identifies them as a priest. Think about a police officer, they wear a style of clothing that identifies them as a cop. Think about someone who is in the military, they wear a style of clothing that identifies them as a soldier. Yes, what they are on the inside is not necessarily all that they present on the outside, but what they wear defines what they have strived to become and from this they set the definition of their life.

How often do you ask yourself, how does the world perceive me? Do others see you and, by how you look and what you wear, can they draw an instant conclusion about who you truly are?

How often do you truly contemplate how you perceive another person? Do you simply see them and decide who you think they are?

What someone thinks you are becomes the definition conceive in the minds of the people who meet you. But, who you are and why you have arrived at this placement in life is far more complex.

If you do not clearly define yourself to yourself—if you do know truly understand how you arrived at who you are in your own mind can you truly know yourself? Moreover, if you are not a clearly defined person what can people conclude when they draw conclusion about you? This is the same when you meet and draw conclusion about others. Is what they project to the world who and what they truly are? Is who and what they are clearly defined in their own minds or are they simply an imposter attempting to be something they truly are not? Moreover, is what you think a person is truly who they are or is what you think they are simply something that you concluded in your own mind but is far from the truth?

Few people truly contemplate the intricacies of their own life. Few people truly contemplate how they actually arrived at being who they are? Do you? Most people, however, are quick to place the judgment of what they think another person is onto that person—be it right or wrong. Do you?

Life is complex. A person's life is very complex. If you do not take the time to know who you truly are and why you have arrived at being who you are, how can anyone else ever truly know you because you do not know yourself? If all you do is think you know who a person is—if all you do is judge who you define that person to be than you have negated who that person truly is because you have not gotten to know the true inner them. Thus, all you have done, from a very egocentric mindset, it to judge who you believe them to be.

First, truly come to know yourself. Second, allow people to be who they truly are, and come to actually know them if you wish. Leave behind judgment in both case, and the world; each person, is allowed to be who they are actually meant to be.

When There Are No Consequences
07/Jan/2021 09:19 AM

How many times in your life have you felt that someone did something wrong to you but they did not suffer any adverse reaction for them doing that evil deed? I believe for most of, at some point in our life, we have experienced times when we felt that way. Maybe we had something stolen, maybe somebody told some lie about us, maybe someone hurt us in some manner—whatever the case, most likely, we have all encountered situations where we were hurt by the actions of others and we felt they suffered no adverse consequences for doing what they did.

Certainly, if we are a conscious individual we must look at it from the other person's point of view. Maybe they did something innocently and it just turned out wrong or maybe they didn't mean it. For them, forgiveness and understanding is the best tool. But, for the majority of life events, when our life, our body, or our possessions are attacked there is one person in the wrong and we all know who they are.

Take a moment and think about your own life. Define one of those moments where you were hurt by the actions of someone else. Were their actions performed in a conscious manner? Did they do what they did with an intended outcome? The answer for most is, yes. A person did what they did knowing or not caring how their actions would hurt your life. So, who is at fault? Without question, they are.

Turn this around for a moment. Think about a time when you hurt someone else. Did you do what you did with intent? If so, why did you do it?

Why did you want to hurt that other person? Why did you want to steal? Why did you want to lie? Why did you want to hit? Why did you want to hurt? Or, why did you not care if you hurt that other person? Really take a few moments and define this in your mind. Why did you do it and what were the consequences to you and to the life of that person who you hurt?

For many, when they are hurt they attempt to strike back. For some, this involves telling their stories and/or reporting the crime.

For most who hurt or damage the life of others, and if they are caught, their response involves making excuses, *"I did what I did because..."* For still others, it involves making up lies—attempting to turn the cause of hurt back around on the other person. But, what is all of this? What does any of this do? Does it change anything or undo the hurt? No, it does not. It simply extenuates the entire process.

It can and should be said that in life we should all be very conscious and knowingly attempt to hurt no one. And, in most cases, as one matures in life, this becomes more and more the coda. Yet, hurt always exists out there. And, hurt is most commonly done by one person to another; no matter how many people are actually involved. In many cases, a person gets away with it. They hurt and they receive no consequences. Then what?

One of the biggest problems in this whole equation is the source of the pain. Who did what to whom and why?

The thing is, there is always one person who exists at the point of inception. There is one person who came up with the idea that eventually leads to hurting someone else. Yes, they are the one to blame. Yes, they are the one who should pay the price for their crime, but do they? In many cases, it does not appear as if they do. Then what?

Now, I could go on about the intricacies of karma and how they will get theirs. But, as I always say, just because a person pays the price for the crime that does not replace or repair the damage to the life of the person they injured. In fact, some people are so wrongfully bold that they take pride in their inflicted injuries and never even think about repairing them.

In life, everybody has a reason for doing what they do. They have a reason that is very logical and sound in their own mind. The hold this reason, they take pride in this reason, and this reason causes them to act, often times in a manner that hurts the life of someone else. They do this until they are stopped. But, stopping someone after they have already done what they have done does not remove the damage that they have caused.

Sure, if you know who the person is who did the bad deed to your life you can go and kick their ass. But, that is illegal. That too is a bad deed. That too may cause you to suffer consequences; legal or otherwise. That is simply you reacting to what someone else has done, thus that person who instigated the bad act in the first place remains in absolute control of the situation.

To begin to find a cure for this situation it must begin with you. Who have you hurt? Have you even tried to repair or erase any hurt you caused? If you have not, how can you focus solely on the hurt inflicted upon you? Thus, no matter how hurt you become at the hands of someone else, if you are not WHOLE enough to see and repair your own wrong doings than why should anyone have any sympathy for you?

Yes, some people may use these words as means to justify their own wrong deeds. But, they are entirely missing the point. Wrong is wrong. Hurt is hurt and you should never do it. If you do hurt someone, intentionally or otherwise, do all you can to fix it. If not, you will forever remain the one at fault.

Who cares about? No really, who cares about you? Right now, take a moment and compose a list of people in your mind that you believe actually care about you. Perhaps your list is long. Perhaps you have very few. But, now comes the next, most important step, truly analyze the list of people you have composed in your mind; do each of those people truly care about you and why?

There is the old saying, *"Blood is thicker than water."* This saying refers to the fact that people who are of the same family, the same bloodline, will more commonly than not stick together. Sure, there are some family members that just hate each other but it is much more common that even if there is conflict within a family, one member doesn't really like another relative, that they will remain in close contact throughout their life. In fact, in most families, the various members will instantly step up to help a family member the moment they need it.

Outside of direct family, however, things get more complicated. So again, take a moment and define the people that you believe care about you outside of your direct family. Ask yourself, *"Why does that person care about me?"* Truly delve into this question. Truly analyses your relationship. Why does that person care about you?

Most commonly, in life, people are drawn to other people via various physical explanations. They like the way they look. They are pretty. They are smart. They can do something for them. They hope to hook up. Being with them will somehow make their life something more than it is without them. But now, think about your own life. Think about someone you once cared about but they are no longer a part of your life. What changed? Why did you let go of your caring? Most probably, they did something you didn't like or they did not give you something that you wanted. Maybe, they weren't the person you initially thought they were or they simply left you behind by one method or another. But, did that person really change or was it simply your perception of them that changed? Why do you no longer care about them?

Now, flip this around. Think about someone that you believed cared about you but has now exited your life. Why did they go? What did you do to drive them away? Or, did they simply reinterpret who you were and what your relationship was and decided it was not beneficial to them so they are gone?

People base their caring about what's in it for them. Again, truly think about it, why do you care about anyone? Again, truly analyze, why does anyone care about you?

If you can be honest with yourself, if you do not allow yourself to fall into relationship illusion, you can chart your path through your life without falling prey to the broken heart syndrome—where someone leaves you alone and heart broken and you do not know why.

People do what they do based upon what is good for themselves. Though many will deny this fact… Though many will lie to themselves about this fact… Though many will tell others that it is not true and they are in it for them… No person remains in a relationship unless there is a need to do so. Yes, this need may be truly messed up, with all kinds of psychological complications attached, but people do what they do to meet a need that they have. Again, why do the people you believe care about you, care about you? If you cannot be honest enough with yourself to truly answer this question, then you are left with a life based in a belief system that can be shattered at any moment simply by a person changing their mind about you.

How Many Times Did You Blow It?
03/Jan/2021 02:03 PM

In each of our lives there are situations where we were offered an opportunity but, for some reason or another, we did not take it—we turned it down. The reason we make these choices are so many that they all cannot even be listed. But, the fact of the matter is, we could have done something but we did not do it and we are left forever understanding that we made the wrong decision.

How about you? How many times did you blow it? How many times were you offered a chance to make your life, your life situation, your life relationship(s), your financial wellbeing, your creative out put, (you name it); how many time were offered a chance but you did not take it?

The thing about life is you only get one chance. Sure, you may get other chances father down the road but they are something different. They are not what you were once offered.

For all of us, there is that something that we had the chance to accept, to do, to live, to experience but we did not do it. What did that not doing mean to the ultimately evolution of your life?

Sure, we can all play philosopher and say, *"It wasn't meant to happen."* But, that's not reality, those are just words. You made a choice and you did not do something, what did that not doing ultimately mean to your life?

I have known people that have come from very humble circumstances and they made the choice to do something and they elevated the level of their life greatly. For some this was done via study and earning the appropriate degree for them to gain credibility in their field. For some this was done by marriage. For others this was done by marriage and then divorce. For certain individuals it was done by focusing on their dream and then meeting and surrounding themselves with the people that could lead them to the plateau they desired. For some it meant doing whatever it took to get them to where they wanted to be. But, no matter where these people progressed their lives towards, the one factor that got them there was that they accepted the opportunity—they took the opportunity that was given to them, they did not turn it down.

Some people define their life by what they did not do. Some people realize their mistake and struggle to regain what they should have done. Others sit back in misery ponding the fact of their bad choice and define their life by what they consider to be their, *"Greatest mistake."* But, this is all Mind Games. It is not doing.

Take a moment right now and define one or more of those situations in your life—those opportunities that you were given but turned down or messed up. Think to those remembrances that periodically come to your mind where you recall that situation or that certain someone that you should have embraced or treated differently. Clearly bring it or them into focus. What was that situation? Who was that person? What did you do to blow it? Why did you blow it?

It's important to not make this an exercise in, *"Whoa is me."* It's also essential that you do not sit there and wallow in your misery about the, *"What you didn't do and how it ruined your life."* Because you did live your life. It was just lived differently than it would have been if you had made a different choice. It is also important not to fantasy about what your life would have been like, *"If only…"* It didn't happen and that is that.

The reason you want to bring one or more of those life-changing moments into focus is that it will reveal to you the nature of your being. It lets you know who you were THEN and perhaps provide you with WHY you find yourself where you find yourself in your life today.

In some case, you can reconstruct Life Situations. You can reach out to the person or persons involved. You can give IT (whatever IT is) another go. Mostly, however, what is gone is gone; the chance you had then you will never have again so you must live with that fact. But, what you really need to do in life, in your life, is to consciously move past your mistakes and come to a new and better understanding of yourself and your life in order that you make clearer, more directed decision in the future.

At any moment of your life everything can change. We can never gage where the next opportunity may come from. But, it is we, the person, who we truly are, that must be ready to take advantage of an opportunity when it is presented to us. To do this, you must be of the right mind and open to the newness and/or the unexpectedness of any new life prospect.

Take a moment or two, look to your mistakes of the past. Seek them out in your mind, remember them, and experience the reason for making the choice you made. Then, move forward/move past that mistake. Consciously make yourself ready for the new, for the next opportunity that comes you way.

Life is a GREAT opportunity. Each day is new. Each day is unexpected. Each day is what you make of it. Allow new opportunities to come into your life. When they do, say, *"Yes."*

The Art and the Impact
of Cultural Appropriation
02/Jan/2021 08:47 AM

When I was young, I had a friend who was a member of what was called, *"The Indian Dance Troupe."* They also had a secondary name, defining their specific group, something like, *"Shoshone Tribe."* What these people did was dress up in these very elaborate costumes with bells and feathers—they dressed the way they believed the Native Americans of long ago would have dressed. The thing was, there was not a Native American among them. Everyone who participated was White. Where they originally got the dances they performed from I do not know but all of these White people would get together, practice, and put on shows mimicking the sounds, the songs, and the dances of a people they had very little true knowledge about.

My friend would always ask me to join the troupe. I always declined. I just felt there was something Not Right about all that was going on.

When I was maybe twelve, we had moved so I changed my Hapkido instruction to a new school. There was a group of Native Americans who attended this school. And though, of course, I was an outsider to their culture, studying with them and befriending them allowed me to have a small view into true Native American Culture in big city America. I was truly glad I never disrespected them by joining that dance troupe.

Around this time, the television series *Kung Fu* came on TV. As we all know, it is a show about a Shaolin Priest/Kung Fu Master who immigrated to America. The thing was, the character was portrayed by a White man pretending to be half

Chinese. Certainly, this TV show has gone down in history as being a positive influence to the spiritual evolution of the Western mind and to the martial arts in general. I too liked the show. But, is what was presented in this TV series historically accurate or was it simply the idealized image of what some person romanticized about a culture, a specific time in history, and a school of the marital arts?

Soon after this time period I entered into the period of my life where I was closely involved with those who practiced Eastern Mysticism. Everyone, including myself, generally wore what we believed to be Eastern style clothing. Though most of us, including myself, were true believers, were we a true part of what actually defined the Eastern understanding of religion and religious knowledge? No, we were not. But, it took me traveling to India (by myself) to come to understand that we were anything but.

People look outside of themselves and their culture to find that something more—that something better that they believe must be out there. They do this because they feel a sense of inadequacy with what they are experiencing. There is always the promise that the culture they focus their intentions upon is or was somehow better— that it/that they know that something more that will fill the hole that some people are experiencing in their lives. The fact is, nothing can give you what you don't have. By its very definition, what you do not have is what you do not have. Yes, the pursuit of other cultures can fill your time, and some my find solace in that, but it will not change your core being. To do that, you must change your definition of the emptiness that you feel within yourself. How do you do that? You become. That does not mean that you try to become something that you are not. What it means is that you become the most you can be, defined by where you find yourself in life, time, and culture.

If you look outside of yourself, hoping to become something that you are not, then you will spend your entire life chasing a false dream. You are what you are. Embrace that and become whole in that knowledge.

When You're Not the One in Charge
01/Jan/2021 02:55 PM

Have you ever been in one of those situations where you must get something done—do it as best as you can do it and you bring someone else onboard to help you but you can tell that they just don't care? I think many of us have encountered situations such as this. This is especially the case when we are the owner of a business or the head of a crew and we must hire someone, as one person alone cannot complete the job, but the person we hire just does not ultimately care about the job they are doing.

When you do a job, whatever that job may be, how focused are you on doing it right? Do you define that job by how much you are getting paid? Do you define that job by what it will do for you life? Do you define that job by how much power or control you are given, leading to how much your ego is being stroked? Or, do you simply look at the job at hand and do it to the absolute best of your ability whether you are getting paid anything or not?

The doing of anything begins with the definition of how willing the person doing the doing is focused upon doing the best job possible. But, how few are the people who are willing to care when they are not the one who will ultimately receive the glory or be blamed at the completion of that job? This is why so few employees truly care about the jobs they do and/or how they treat other workers or customers because its just a job. They are there to get paid. If they do a bad job and get fired maybe they may get angry but it will never be them who will pay the ultimate price if a business fails and must be closed down or the job at hand is never completed.

I know from a personal perspective, I have been very lucky with many of the people I have brought on to compete the films I have made. But, every now and then, there is that one person who really comes onboard with the intention of either not caring or actually trying to harm the process. As in all life situations, one may question, *"Why?"* But, in actuality, the answer is quite clear and quite simply; it is not their project so they just don't care.

In life, we are all cast to being interactive with other people. In life, we are all destine to work for or have others work for us. We can hope, in these life situations, that the other person will care about the completion of that anything as much as we do, but it is unlikely that will always be the case. Sad, but true.

What is the answer to this life dilemma? The first thing is we must try to surround ourselves with those of like mind who truly care about the task at hand. But, some people, by their very nature, are deceptive. They lie and they pretend. They deny any responsibility anytime that they are called to task. Due to this fact, no matter how much you expect from a person, that expectation may never be met because there is no guarantee that when it comes time for them to truly step up to the plate that they will be willing to what is required of them.

Ultimately, most people only care about themselves. They are only defined by what is on their mind, what is in their mind, and what emotions and programming are controlling their mind. Meaning, a person is what they are and you can never make them anything more. If they care about you, great! If they care about their job, great! If they care about other people: the customers, the fans, great! If not, there is nothing you can do to change their focus and make them into the person you believed or you hoped they would be.

As you walk through life choose you friends, your associates, your workers, and your care givers carefully because when it comes time to complete the task at hand they are the only one you can truly rely upon. If they don't care, they don't care. If they only care about themselves, they only care about themselves.

Be the kind of person who cares. Be the kind of person who, when you are asked to do something, (for pay or otherwise), that you see the purpose of your mission and do that job with the integrity that is require to get it done right.

Be that right person. Be that caring person. Be that person who gets the job done right.

*   *   *

01/Jan/2021 02:54 PM

Saying you're sorry doesn't change the damage that you've caused.

I imagine that there is not one person out there who has not been going through their day, perhaps quite happily, when all of sudden someone else forces their way into your Life Experience and really brings you down. Maybe they do this in a small way or maybe they do this in a big way. But, one way or the other, what they have done is to truly kill your buzz, bring you down, and removing any peace, joy, or happiness that you may be feeling.

When these situations occur, they usually do so quite shockingly. Meaning, you don't see them coming. For it is certain that you do not want them to happened and if you had a choice you would not allow them to happen. But, BAM, out of nowhere, they do happen.

On the end of the recipient, these situations are most commonly totally unexpected. For the person who instigates them, however, sometimes they are anything but.

There are certain people out there who want to force their way into a person's life. They want to get a reaction. Why, is anyone's guess? But, there is a certain subset of people who want to alter the Life Path of someone else in a less than ideal manner. Not good! That is a clear definition of a Not Good Person. But, those people are out there.

Mostly, however, these situations come out of nowhere. They occur via the unconscious action(s) of the perpetrator. For example, I think to a couple of times where my car was rear-ended by the driver behind me messing around with his phone. From that, BAM. A total good experience killer.

Here in California, it is actually illegal to have your phone in your hand while driving. But, look around, there are many-many people who still do.

One of these situations occurred, a couple of years ago, when my lady and I were rear-ended. I was riding in the passenger seat of her car. We were happily driving home from this new boutique ice cream shop and BAM, an Uber driver, on his phone, powerfully hit us from behind, as he did not realize he was coming up to a stoplight. Her car was totaled. A car she really liked. Thus, gone was our moment of ice cream induced happiness, leading to dealing with all of the dealing-with of a crashed car and buying a new one, and all that, all because someone was behaving in an unconscious manner.

Most, *"Harsh Your Mellow,"* situations are not that intense. But, they are nonetheless instigated by the unconscious action(s) of someone else and then fueled by specific personality traits of the instigating individual.

For example, I was at Starbucks yesterday. I pretty much go to Starbucks everyday. I did a mobile app order as I tend to do in these days of the pandemic. I walked in and was happily greeted by some of the baristas who know me. They gave me my latte but my bagel was not ready. Unusual, but I was told it would be coming soon. No big deal. As I was standing there, in walks this barista I had never seen before. I have to be politically correct here, but as it is important to the storyline, I need to describe this individual. This was one of those people in transition; I believe from male to female. The person was tall with their blonde hair tightly tied back. As they checked into their job, on the store's iPad, they looked over in my direction and gave me a really harsh look. Why? I have no idea. I never saw them before. But, they did. Anyway, after several minutes of waiting, and still no bagel, I walked over to the young man who was doing that type of thing behind the counter and inquired about my bagel. He looked at me and said they didn't have anymore everything bagels, which is what I had ordered. My question to him was, *"Why didn't you tell me?"* The aforementioned person, who wasn't part of this conversation, immediately went off on me, telling me I wasn't being nice, why wasn't I kind, etc, etc., etc... My thought was, *"How is asking a person why you didn't tell me about my bagel, while leaving me standing there for who knows how long, being anything negative?"* The barista was totally making a scene, completely ruining my Starbuck experience. I could have exchanged words with them, but that is exactly what people like this want. They want to ruin your experience, and drag you into melodrama, all dominated by whatever is going on in their mind. Their mind, not yours. Me, I just left without my bagel.

So, this is the thing in life, we are all going to experience those moments. Those moments where someone comes out of nowhere and really takes away any joy you are feeling, pushing you down the path of non-happiness. The question you have to ask yourself is, *"When these moments occur what are you going to do about it? How are you going to behave?"*

In most of these situations, once they are done, they are done. There is nothing that you can do to change what has been done. The only thing that you actually have control over is how you react. How you do decide to react defines who you are as a person and what will occur next in your life, based upon the situation that you were handed but had no desire in creating.

Can you smile when you are upset? If you can, that may be the best medicine. Can you turn and leave when someone says something wrong, foolish, mean, or untrue to you? If you can, that may be the best medicine.

The main thing to do when these situation befall you is to not allow yourself to be dragged into them. That is what the instigator wants. They want to get a reaction out of you. They want to control your emotions and your life. Again, why? Who knows? But, they do. They want to take control over you, your thoughts, your emotions, and your reactions. If you start to argue with them, they have won. If you punch them, they have won. But, if you say nothing and walk away then you have taken back the control over your life and you have won. You may be annoyed, angry, pissed off, or just not happy but you have not given away the control of your life.

Never let the people who want to take away your happiness gain control over your life.

I was having a discussion about Japan, Korea history and the evolution of the Japanese martial arts with one of my colleagues the other day. He mentioned that he had read this Master's Thesis on the subject where the author had referenced one of my books. He pulled it up and showed me the segment. It was interesting to read how one person had interpreted my writings. What he did was to take my research on a subject and then put his own spin on it. Certainly, all that is part and particle of the academic world. People find the research previously composed on a subject and then draw their own collusions based upon the amalgamation of their research and the writings of others.

For anyone who has walked down the path of academia you will understand that it takes time to find previously composed research on a subject, study it, and then find works that help present your own point of view and conclusions. In fact, the more previously composed works you sight in your paper, or in this case Thesis, the more likely it is that your instructor or Thesis Committee Members will find your work compelling.

I truly suggest that anyone out there take a class where research and writing is required and then really take the time to deeply research a subject and compose a documented paper. It truly opens up an entirely new realm of life-understanding as it causes you to be forced to explore the understandings of others.

There is a problem in all of this, however. And, this was one of the subjects of my colleague and my discussion. That problem is, perceived and presented rationalizations. The fact is, people want to present any understanding that they believe they understand from their own point of view. In fact, that is what the composition of a Thesis or a Dissertation actually entails; the study of previously composed documentation on a specific subject combined with individualized research into order to present a new and unique understanding about a topic defined and rationalized by the mind of the student. The key premise in all of this is, however, an individual's personal point of view. One person studying what has previously been documented and then finding the appropriate texts to support their own point of view.

But, what is a point of view? Is a point of view fact or is it personal perception? If one truly contemplates this subject, the answer is obvious. Yet, there it is, all of this information being present in a Thesis as fact, based upon all of the previously prepared research, that was also presented as fact, that has been published in books, and then conglomerated by the student hoping to present the topic in the way they perceive the subject.

One of the things I do in life is critique the writings presented to publishers from authors in hopes of acquiring a book deal. I think back to this one manuscript I was asked to read by this one publisher. It was a book on the history of the Korean martial arts. Just as my colleague and I were discussing, you cannot understand the Japanese or the Korean martial arts without understanding the history and the evolution of both of these cultures and ancient systems of combat.

The manuscript I was given was full of quotes from other previously published books and writings, including my own, on the subject. But, what overpowered all of this author's research was personal opinions leading to, in some cases, false conclusions. This is where the problem arises in not only academic document creation but in the works of all authors, including myself.

As an author, specificity in the realms of non-fiction, you are asked to present a specific subject in a specific manner that then may be consumed by the reader. In many cases, you are asked to present the subject in a manner that was prescribed by an editor. Thus, you must meet their requirements if you hope to have the book published. This is the same in the world of academia, what you write must be written in a manner that will be accepted by those people judging your writings. What does this all lead to? What it leads to is expected and acceptable conclusions.

All writing, by all people, whether they are academically trained or not, is defined by a point of view. That point of view may or may not be based upon a very prescribed set of parameters, dictated by someone other than the author or not. But, whatever the case, there is a set of rules that must be followed either in the publishing or the academic world.

What does this leave us with? It leaves us with a world of writings based upon a prescribed set of expected standards combined with a person's personal opinion. Meaning, all things that you read must be understood to be less than one-hundred truthful and valid as they are composed by the mind of one or more individuals presenting a specific subject from a prescribed point of view.

The person's Thesis that I just mentioned interpreted my writings to suit his own needs. Were his quotes of my work construed as I had meant them to be understood? No, they were not. They were his interpretations of my research. They were him defining my writings (as others) based upon his own individualize perception. Thus, though his Thesis was a work of supposed history, was it? Or, was it simply his decided upon perception of history?

All life is defined by what you think. All life is defined by what the person next to you thinks. Do you think the same thing? Probably not. Moreover, what do you base your thinking upon? Is it true research that you personally investigated? Or, is it simply opinion with documentation, presented as fact, composed by the mind of a person with a prescribed point of view to present?

One really needs to question anyone's presentation of knowledge. Because is what they are saying truth or is what they are saying simply their interpretation of someone else's opinion based upon the previously composed research of someone else who is also presenting the subject based upon their own point of view?

Purpose Verse Intent
and the Why a Person Does What They Do
30/Dec/2020 07:29 AM

The Sanskrit word, *"Varta,"* is the translation of the English word, "Purpose." More exactly, *"Varta,"* describes someone with a firm purpose as to what they hope to achieve. The Sanskrit word, *"Kardatha,"* defies someone having a very specific or highly defined goal.

If we look to the world, if you look to yourself, how many people have a very specific goal—a very designated endpoint that they hope to achieve? Yes, most everyone has a daydream, *"Divasvapna,"* that something that they wish they could achieve, but how few are the people that set a clear path to its achievement?

Though there are several words that can be used to translate the English word, *"Purpose,"* into the Sanskrit language, perhaps the most commonly used word is, *"Azaya."*

A person's purpose is why they are attempting to make something happen in their life and/or the life of other people. Now, this is where one of the primarily elements of Life Accomplishment comes into play and how it affects the overall evolution of the individual. Why is a person doing what they are doing? What do they hope to achieve?

If we look to the person who is centered onto themselves, and if they possess a clear purpose, they hope to achieve something to make themselves that something more—they hope to achieve and become that something that they consider better. Though one may argue that this style of, *"Purpose,"* is based in ego and therefore by that very definition it removes a person from following the Higher Path of consciousness, it is nonetheless a clear purpose. Thus, they hold a clear intent.

Many people in this world place their focus outside of themselves. They define their life by what and who is outside of them. They do not focus on making themselves that something more—becoming that better, more accomplished, and fulfilled individual, instead they want to do something that affects the life of someone else. Some people do this a mean of helping others, while others do it as a mean to hurt others. Though one of these pathways is obviously of the higher calling, they both have one primary foundational element; they cause a person to place their focus outside of themselves. Thus, all that is done will not and cannot cause that person to find a Higher State of Self. At best, all any of their actions can do is to provide that person with a sense of elation. Therefore, all they are ultimately doing is taking a drug. The drug of doing something to or for someone else that makes them feel a specific kind of sensation.

Each individual has the choice to make about what they do with their life. Some people set a clear goal at becoming the best person that they can be. Others hope to become revered in the eyes of others. While still others hope to influence the life of people outside of themselves in either a positive or a negative manner. The question that few people ask themselves, however, is why are they doing what they are doing; what is their purpose and what is their internet?

To truly understand life, to truly understand your life, and to truly come to a clear conclusion about why you are living what you are living and why you have encountered what you have encountered as you have passed through your life, you must come to understand your self-proclaimed purpose and your self-defined intent.

Take a moment right now and think about it. Clearly bring into your mind what is your purpose and what is your intent. Why have you done what you have done? Why are you about to do what you are about to do?

Whatever your answer is that is your answer. There are no right or wrong answers. But, if you have truly investigated your motivational pathway not only will you have done something that few people ever take the time to understand but you will also have come to a much clearer conclusion about who you are, why you are, and what you can expect to happen next in your life.

Each person is defined by their purpose and their intent. What are yours?

29/Dec/2020 04:06 PM

A replica is never the original.

Cutting the Line for the COVID Vaccine
29/Dec/2020 07:20 AM

A little over a week ago, the first and then the second vaccine(s), promised to combat the COVID-19 pandemic this earth is facing, were released. As expected, there have been problems getting the vaccine out to the people. Last night on CNN I heard that only about ten percent of the vaccines that have been distributed have gotten out to the people in the first tier of recipients; namely first responders, hospital doctors and nurses, and the elderly living in retirement communities. That's what I thought would happen. There is no plan.

I know a lot of people out there don't trust and/or do not want to receive the vaccine. I get it. What are they shooting into our arms? And, what are the long-term side effects? Who knows??? But, it is the only hope we have right now. This pandemic has devastated the earth and destroyed the lives of so many people. I too have been affected, like so many-many others.

Yesterday, I was told about this person... I'm trying to find the best way to say who she is... It's complicated... Let's leave it at she is someone fairly close to me. In any case, is she a first responder: an EMT, a paramedic, a fireman, or a policeman? No. Is she a doctor or a nurse who must deal with the horrendous amount of people flooding the hospitals with COVID-19 everyday? No. Is she someone like a grocery store worker, a department store clerk, a Starbucks barista, or a bank teller who must go face-to-face with people everyday to pay their rent? No. What she is, is a person in a high-powered position of authority at the corporate level of a large hospital chain. But, does she go into the hospitable everyday? No, she does not. Like so many others she has been working from home for the past nine months. Yet, due to her position, she was one of the first to get the vaccine. This truly made me angry.

She has a very unique name and there was a part of me that thought to put it out there on the internet and tell the world what she did, as it would be very easy for the internet hordes to seek her out. But, that's just not the kind of person that I am.

The fact is, what she did was and is wrong. She cut the line. She got the vaccine when so many others, who truly need it, have not. I see on the news that, here in L.A., there are many nurses protesting because they can't get the vaccine yet the must go into the ER everyday hoping to save the lives of others. Yet, there she was, a person with power, thoughtlessly thinking of no one else but herself, and getting the vaccine before so many others, who truly need it, have not received it as of yet. That is just wrong!

After I found this out last night, (and was fairly pissed), I was asked, *"Wouldn't you get the vaccine right now if you could?"* My answer, *"In a perfect world, where everyone was being vaccinated, of course I would. But here, now, where the people who really need it can't even get vaccinated, no I would not. I would give my dose to someone who really deserves it."*

So, this is life. There are people in the position of power. There are people who do not even think about anyone else when they do what they do as long as they can cut the line, get to the front, and get what they want before anyone else. It's not right, but that is just the way it is. But, it shouldn't be. People should have more care for their

250

fellow human beings than this but for many, as with the case of the person just described, they do not.

For the rest of us, I hope the vaccine distribution program improves. But again, they have no plan, so I don't know how it can. First we were told, twenty-million people would be vaccinated by the end of the year. We are now like three days away from the end of the year and only a small fraction, (about ten percent), of that have been vaccinated. This, while people are getting sick, people are dying, people are losing their livelihoods, all while some insignificant, selfish person, cuts the line and gets vaccinated when so many more deserving people should have gotten it long before her. Sad… What's also sad is that she will probably never read this, as I am sure she doesn't read this blog. No one will ever tell her how truly selfish and wrong she is. So, she will simply walk the path of her life, selfishly and uncaringly oblivious to the damage she has done. The person she took that vaccination from may die. Then what will be her karma? How many people are there like this person? Are you one of them?

Many people, when they encounter an individual that they consider to be of a more advanced or more revered position in life than themselves, remove Self-Definition and replace it with a deflection of responsibility. *"My teacher says…"* In the various ways these words are presented, the individual references the fact that they have a teacher, that they are a student, and that they have been guided by someone else. From this, they remove all layers of culpability and thereby are not ultimately responsible for what they say or what they do.

There is a very large problem with this mindset, however. That problem is, the person who deflects Personal Knowledge can never become the Master of their own destiny. They can never be the one that others turn to for True Knowledge as they, themselves, are proclaiming that they do not personally possess it.

Look to someone who has passed through their life and has obtained a position of authority. If you study their journey you will see that, yes, they did study a specific pathway of understand but then they emerged at the other end of that journey with a clear sense of Self Actualized truth. Yes, they were taught. Yes, they learned. But, at the end of their course of study they emerged as the True Knower of what they understand.

No matter how much a person studies and learns from another individual, it is they who translates that knowledge into Personal Understanding. If all a person does is to mirror what he or she is taught they can never become a Master of their craft. It is only the person who learns, understands, and masters whatever subject they are studying that emerges as the individual who is understood to hold the True Knowledge of what they speak.

Whenever you meet someone, truly listen to the words they speak. Truly study the source of their knowledge and who and what they claim as a source. If all a person does is speak their mind, with no basis for advanced understanding, they should not be listened to because all they are driven by is ego. If a person deflects what they say by claiming what they speak and what they teach is based upon the knowledge that someone else possess then instead of learning from them go to the source of their knowledge for that is obviously the person that holds the True Knowledge.

In life, few people Know and the ones who claim that they do usually do not, they simply pretend that they do.

Be careful whom you listen to and from whom you study. If they do not truly Know, you can never Know, as what they have to teach you is, at best, Borrowed Knowledge.

If you don't turn on the stove nothing will ever get cooked.

*   *   *

24/Dec/2020 08:17 AM

The question you must ask yourself in all life situations, is it getting better or is it getting worse?

The answer to that question will let you know what you need to do.

Late into the Late Night
23/Dec/2020 01:42 PM

I was kicking around late into the late night, last night. Which is something that I tend to do. In times gone past, I used to spend the late nights at nightclubs. I did that way longer than I probably should have. I was deep into my forties when I finally let them go. Now, currently, with all the COVID-19 stuff going on and all that, and everything being closed by order of the powers-that-be, I tend to spend the late nights flipping channels on TV when I'm not in the creative mode of doing something.

Speaking of those days of yore, a friend of mine sent me the link to a 2015 article written about one of my late night haunts of way back in the way back when the other day. They place was called, *Zero Zero*.

My buddy Venchinzo and I would hit there after slam dancing at the *Starwood* or the *Whiskey* or playing a gig at *Madam Wong's* or the *Hong Kong Café* in Chinatown. We would grab a bottle of Jack on the way that I would stash into the pocket of my sport coat and we would sit back in the darkness of the club and let the evening roll on drinking the nasty, junkyard beer they passed out for free, intermingled with taking hits off of the bottle. We would generally leave as dawn was approaching. I would drop Venchinzo off at his place in Hollywood and I would head back to my place in Hermosa, usually arriving just as the sun was coming up. I could tell you all kinds of stories of the goings on of that place, in fact, I probably have in some forgotten piece of poetry or prose, but a paragraph from the aforementioned article by

Greg Renoff probably says it best, *"Out of these conversations came one of Hollywood's most underappreciated cultural landmarks, the Zero Zero Club. Within weeks of its summer 1980 debut, the Zero Zero became the late-night destination for everyone who was anyone on the city's wide-ranging punk scene. As the club's reputation grew in the Hollywood underground, celebrities came to haunt the Zero Zero as well, making for late night scenes where upstart punkers and aspiring artists rubbed elbows with stars like actor John Belushi and Van Halen frontman David Lee Roth. This kind of social leveling produced gatherings where the coolest, rather than the most famous, people in town could come together to carouse and network until dawn. As former Zero Zero bartender Pleasant Gehman explains, 'It was like going to Studio 54, without the velvet ropes. If you knew about a place like this, it meant that you were hip enough to go to it, and so it didn't matter if you were a celebrity or not a celebrity.'"*

I just checked and found that there are a couple of good online articles about the place. Search 'em out if you feel like it...

Anyway, that was then this is now...

Flipping channels last night, I came upon the James Bond flick, *License to Kill.* Though not one of the stand out James Bond films, by my appraisal, it did feature by *Roller Blade Seven* costar, Don Stroud. For that reason alone I was drawn into re-watching it.

You know, it kind of made me think... Don Stroud, a GREAT, very respected actor, did that film in 1989. Well, they probably shot it a year earlier in 1988, as it usually takes about a year for an A-Film to be released after it is shot. The next year, in 1990, I got to meet Don Stroud on the set of one of the first films I worked on, *The Confessional,* which later was released as, *Divine Enforcer.* The next year, I got to work with him on, *The Roller Blade Seven.*

Stroud was always one of my favorite actors, from my youth forward. Why he stepped down from his plateau to work on such low budget films, I can only guess. But, I'm glad and thankful that he did and that I got to met him and work with him. Truly, one of the high points of my acting career. Great guy!

The point being, in all of our lives, one thing leads to another. What you do now will equal what you will be allowed to do in the future. If your vision for your destiny is clear, you can make things happen. Hell, if your vision is unclear, things still can happen but they are just far less likely to bring you to moments of intersective perfection.

I have known people from the Midwest that have come to L.A., with no true idea about the Hollywood system, yet they moved forward and made movies with some of their idols. They had the focus that made it happen. More often than not, however, I have known people who have come to Hollywood with a wild dream but were never willing to take the steps to make that dream a reality. They either did not allow their dream to materialize because of ego, being holier than thou, thinking they were too good to be humble and do jobs that were below their envisioned reality, or they bite the hand that could feed them. All of that leads to a life not fully actualized by not allowing the perfection of living the perfect moment that can happen if you are in alignment with the cosmic forces of the universe where unexpected dreams can become a reality.

Sure, most of us are not going to co-star in a James Bond film. Though most, including myself, wish that we could. But, if we allow ourselves to flow into the process of perfect evolution we then may get to work with that person that we always held a lot of respect for who was a co-star in a James Bond film. You get what I'm saying... All we have to be is receptive to the process that can place us in a position of receiving.

So, know your dream. Take the steps to make it a reality. And, even if you never climb to the pinnacle of the plateau that you hoped to inhabit, if you embrace your path with knowing humbleness than maybe, just maybe, you can scratch the surface of that dream you hold and live just a little bit of what you hoped to achieve.

*　　*　　*

Should you write poetry if no one is going to read it?

You Only Have a Moment to Make a Difference
22/Dec/2020 02:58 PM

There is this spider that lives inside of the mirror on the driver's side of my lady's car. We know this because there always seems to a spider web surrounding the mirror. Even after we wash the car, a few days later it reappears.

Though we always assumed there was a sider inside of the mirror, we never saw it. We never saw it until last weekend.

We were driving out in the Valley and she got a flat tire. As we were going to meet someone, I didn't want to get dirty so we called up AAA to change the tire. As we were waiting for AAA to arrive, there he was, the spider came out. He extended his web a bit and dropped down from the mirror. The fact was, it was kind of fun to finally see him.

We spoke about the spider and his antics for a moment or two and then I got the idea that this would probably be a good time to set him free. ...At least free him from us and my lady's mirror.

I was on the passenger side. I got out of the car and walked around the car but by the time I got to the driver's side, he had disappeared. He had re-hidden to his home in the mirror. Had I been a moment or two sooner, had we not discussed his existence, had I not thought about it, I could have gotten there in time. But, I did not.

The moral of the story; you only have a moment to make a difference. If you don't do what you need to do immediately, then your chance to make a difference may be lost forever.

I was sitting out on my patio last evening, looking out over the ocean and sipping a cup of tea, as I like to do. The sun had already set but its rays still etched the colors of red and orange onto the horizon. The rest of the sky was grey as the night was coming on.

Up, over to my left, I could see what they are calling, *The Christmas Star.* An occurrence that has not happened for eight hundred years where Jupiter and Saturn closely aligned. I took out my binocular and checked it out. I know a lot of the people I have on the peripheries of my life were all into this occurrence—seeing all kinds of spiritual and energy ramifications, but I didn't really feel a flux in anything.

In any case, I was sitting there, enjoying the evening, when out of the corner of my eye I saw a shooting star. It really surprised me because the sky was not yet dark and aside from the Christmas Star, there weren't really any other stars that could be seen in the sky.

I know when you see a shooting star you are suppose to make a wish. At least that is the old wives tale. So, that thought did cross my mind. But, I realized, I didn't want to waste my wish. Right there, in that moment, everything was okay.

You know, we all wish something in our life was different. Certainly, I have a long list of things that I would like to change and improve. I have things, situations, and people that cause my life to be less than perfect—at least less than perfect in my mind's eye. So, if I wanted to pull out a wish from my long list, I could. But, every now and then, if we can let go and relax, seek nothing more than what we have, sit back into the perfection, we can actually embrace a small dose of Satori. We can actually feel the perfection of the perfect moment. Sure, if we want to focus on what is wrong with our life we can find the flaws. But, if we let go, sit back, relax, look out onto the horizon, take a sip from our cup of tea, we can each experience the experience that all is well with our world.

Thanks for the Publicity.
Thanks for the Misinformation.
21/Dec/2020 10:00 AM

There is a certain subset of my friends who are filmmakers. Just like with any group of friends that follow a specific religion, they are going to talk about the god that they worship. Me… Filmmaking is kind of like the martial arts… It is something that I do but it is not something that I am. Other people, however, they are devout; filmmaking is all that they think about. I appreciate people like that; whatever god they worship… They are the true believers. It is all they think about equaling all that they do.

I was hanging out with one such friend the other day. A true filmmaker. As filmmaking is virtually all that they think about, filmmaking, and its general vast expansiveness, is all that they search out online.

We're hanging out and they want to show me a couple of reviews/discussions about me and my Zen Films they have found online. Me… I just never seek that kind of stuff out. I don't want to know! Good or bad, positive or negative; whatever… It's all somebody else's ideas about what they think went on but it's all in their head. They weren't there, they don't know anything as fact—they never spoke to me, they don't know my motivations or my parameters, so how can they know anything about anything? Yet, they write or they speak.

I was shown the stuff my friend had discovered. I thought the things said were funny. Mostly wrong, but funny.

264

I have seen it written that some people claim that I don't like negative reviews. Again, how do they know? They don't know me. They've never spoken to me. They've never contacted and asked me anything about anything. Yet, they make claims.

Do you ever contemplate that? Why people make claims about somebody/anybody else without knowing them personally? Anyway, before I get off subject…

True, I don't like it when people break copyright law and use my stuff without permission, but reviews: good or bad, I could care less… I care more about the case, (and I have said this a lot of times before), that people put their ideas out there as fact when they are far-far from the truth. Come on, we all know it… There's a lot of misinformation on the internet. Why believe anything you hear or read?

Anyway… With that part of our adventure behind us, we sat down to watch a couple of films. As my friend is a true, *"Filmmaker,"* all they think about is film and all that, we then watched the documentary: *Hearts of Darkness: A Filmmaker's Apocalypse.* It's a great doc about Coppola and the making of *Apocalypse Now.* I hadn't seen that film in many-many years. It was a good watch. Then, we watched the comedy, *Living in Oblivion,* about an indie filmmaker who runs into a lot of problems. It features Steve Buscemi, Catherine Keener, and Dermot Mulroney among others. Good movie. That one initially got past me back in '95. Never saw it before. It documents a lot of the nonsense that may take place on the set of an indie film. Something that few of these reviewers of Scott Shaw and other indie filmmakers and films have any true idea about as they have never actually made a film or tried to play the Hollywood game. Again, leading to my understanding, if you don't know how can you know?

The doc, but more intensively the film, made be laugh because it all just goes to the reality of the reality of filmmaking and how the true creator of any film must deal with so much; so many unexpected variables to get 'er done. …Something that the reviewer will never understand.

It made me think back to a time when I was teaching a course on independent filmmaking at U.C.L.A. The movie, *Bowfinger,* (also about the crazy world of independent filmmaking, from a very comedic perspective), had just come out and some of my students kept referring to my declarations about filmmaking and my proclaimed methods of filmmaking were mirroring much of what was in the film. I hadn't yet seen the film yet but once I did I totally understood what they were saying.

That's the thing about indie filmmaking, you got to get out there and do it—do it by whatever means possible. You're not necessarily intending it to be some great high budget epic like *Apocalypse Now,* (which was also an indie film, just a very high budgeted indie film), but you are attempting to get your vision onto whatever medium you are shooting on. As Francis Ford Coppola proclaims, in essence, at the end of, *Hearts of Darkness, "Some fat girl with her fathers camcorder will be the one to make the next great film."* And, that's the reality that has come to pass. Though he didn't foresee it then, none of us did, but now you can make a great movie on your phone. You just have to get out there and do it. No, it may not be what the critics like or expect, but that it is not to say that it will not push the boundaries of art. And, that is what independent filmmaking, (or any other creation of art), is all about: doing it, creating it, making it happen, and seeing it through to its completion. That is true art.

To the critics... Thanks for the publicity, thanks for the misinformation. But, you know, instead of thinking that you know—instead of interpreting what you see, why don't you have the integrity to go to the source and discus any film or filmmaker you are planning to do a piece about with the person at the source of that film directly? If nothing else, you will be getting closer to the truth and will not become just another person trying to get your own name and your own face out there while spreading misinformation to an internet world that is already overwhelmed with it.

To everyone else, get out there and make art. Create art, whatever art you envision. For that is truly giving something to the world.

*   *   *

20/Dec/2020 12:11 PM

How much of this moment are you going to remember?

How much of this moment are you going to live fully?

When you are reading a holy scripture do you ever ponder the path that text took to be placed in front of your eyes?

Let's take the Bible for example. The Bible went through a very long process of translations and adaptations to reach the state it is in today. Here, now, at this point in history, one can find many versions of the Bible presented for the public to read in numerous languages. Is the sourcepoint of these manuscripts the same? Yes, most probably, but if you read the words in these proclaimed scriptures each of these editions are presented in their own unique manner. Does this make one version of the Bible less and another one more? That is open to individualized interpretation. But, the fact is, yes, they are different. So, which one is a true Bible?

Historians have charted the way in which the Bible came into existence so I won't go into that here. But, all one has to do is to look to the history of the evolution of the Bible and they will easily find that it evolved in a very haphazard manner dominated by the people and the powers of eras gone past. Thus, is the Bible a creation of god or is it a creation of man?

The Christian is taught that one must have faith. But, they are also taught that their specific brand of the teaching is the best—better than the others. Thus, two branches of Christianity, though based in the same religious origin, may be interpreted very differently.

If we look to books like the Tao Te Ching, which was a big influence on my life, we see that virtually every copy you pick is translated somewhat differently. Yes, Chinese, and particularly ancient Chinese, is a very interpretive written language but two books claiming the same source, origin, and truth are vastly different when they are compared. Is one the true teachings and the other is not? Again, this is open to personal speculation.

Christians are taught that they simply must believe, that they must give their life over to, *"Faith."* Meaning, you must believe what you are taught to believe. But, who are you taught by and why? Why must you believe simply because you are expected to believe?

Life and particularly spiritual life and spiritual realization are based upon personal inquiry. Inquiry of the self and inquiry of the greater cosmos, leading to communion with the absolute power of reality. If one does not question the sourcepoint for their knowledge all they become is a vehicle of belief. But, belief is never fact, it is never self-realization. Thus, if you simply take the words of any scripture as fact simply because it is printed and placed into front of your eyes to read then you are allowing whomever put those words together to be the guiding guardian of your life.

How many people claiming holiness—how many people claiming knowingness have been proven to not be true to the teachings they teach? With this simply fact as a basis, it should cause anyone who walks the path of religious spirituality to question the source of their printed knowledge as, at best, it is simply a concoction and a translation of some person's interpretation of what they believe should be presented to the world.

Read, but always question what you are reading because there are no words written that have not been composed with an intended purpose of causing a person to believe a specific point of view. All words can be traced back to a man (or woman). All people are fallible. Thus, be careful of being guided by what you believe based on what you have read because all people hold an agenda and if they used so-called Holy Scriptures to get you to do something all of their proclamations and requests should be held suspect.

The Flashback Documentary
19/Dec/2020 07:40 AM

I don't know about you but during this pandemic I've been watching a lot of TV. You can't really go anywhere. Things are either closed via edict of the government or the infection rate is just too high. Can't go sit down and have a nice meal at a restaurant. Closed. Can't go have a drink (or three) at a bar. Closed. Can't travel. No country will let people from other countries in without (at least) a long quarantine period. Can't go to the gym as they are either closed or they are touted as having a very high infection rate. Etc, etc… Luckily, I have my own workout space but I don't feel comfortable opening the doors to others as I don't want it to be a vector for the transmission of the disease as the infection rate is so high here in California. Thus, a lot of unrequited free time equaling a lot of TV.

Me, I have always enjoyed watching documentaries. Just like I enjoy reading autobiographies; you can really learn a lot about a specific individual. One of the things I have noticed that has been recently taking place, in the production of documentaries, is that what a filmmaker will do is sit the person of focus down in front of the camera, interview them, and then intermix the interview with stock footage. Though this may provide a nice opportunity for the subject to tell their side of the story, this style of documentary filmmaking just seems so lethargic. I mean, aside from going to stock film houses, film vaults, and film libraries, there is very little work that is put into the project.

You might expect this style of documentary filmmaking to be done by a film student or even a network where an actor or news anchor has worked for many years. But, what I find, more times than not, is that this style of flashback documentary creation is being made by experienced, and in some cases, celebrated filmmakers. Now, I am not saying I do not watch these documentaries and in some circumstances enjoy them and learn from them but it just all seems so indolent.

Remember when documentaries presented new, unseen, undiscovered, self-created footage? That's what I am speaking about; documentaries that cut new ground, that pushed the envelope of knowledge, understanding, and cinema as a whole.

So... This is not a criticism, this is just a conclusion; a depiction of an era where things have changed as I suppose they always do. A time when things that are not done with a creatively high level of excellence are accepted as everyone (like myself) has just been watching way too much TV.

Watching Movies You Don't Like
18/Dec/2020 01:41 PM

I was driving down PCH today listening to this radio program on one of the local NPR stations. Each Friday they do this film review segment. Sometimes it's really informative because they periodically discuss movies that are totally under the radar; along with many of the mainstream releases. I've been pointed in the direction of a few very interesting films…

You know, during this time of the COVID-19 Coronavirus Pandemic, with all of its lockdowns, etc., there has been a lot of talk of COVID fatigue. I can't imagine how hard it must be for young students to be kept away from their friends, their group gatherings, their proms, their graduation ceremonies, and all that. Or, to have to learn remotely, especially if your family isn't set up with highly functioning internet access. Or, to be one of those parents with your kids at home for months upon months. Or, the people who have lost their jobs because so many businesses have been forced to close and they don't have enough food to feed themselves or their family. Those people, and others, are the ones who are really paying a very high price for this China induced epidemic. But, as for me, my COVID fatigue has been watching bad movies…

Now, I've got access to so many stations and streaming services it isn't even funny. Fios, Netflix, Showtime, Epix, Starz, HBO Max, Amazon Prime, Apple TV, you name it… But, what has really come to haunt me is how many bad movies there are out there. …At least movies I find to be bad. Sometimes, I scan the stations for an hour or more just trying to find something I'm willing to watch.

My lady isn't like that. She can watch bad films. She is so much more forgiving than I. Whenever we are in our pods on one of those long international flights, she watches movie after movie. Once I've gone through a couple, I just lay back in meditative semi-sleep consciousness because I just don't wanna see things I don't wanna see.

The point to this little ditty is... So often, when I am listening to film reviewers, they just sit there and bag the movie they are reviewing. They hate A LOT of the movies they have to watch. Me, I just can't imagine that kind of life. How can you spend the hours of your days, (as few as those hours of life actually turn out to be), watching something that you hate? I mean, shouldn't you only be doing things that make you happy as much as possible?

I get it; some people pay their rent by reviewing movies. Most people aren't like that, however. Just look at the reviews of movies on the internet; how many people hate what they watch? If you hate it, why watch it? Even if you're a professional reviewer, why watch something/anything you hate? If you don't like it, turn it off! That's what I do. Life isn't a competition for watching movies you don't like.

This has just been my thoughts on the subject... My advice, spend your Life Time doing things you like, watching things you appreciate, and living. Because, sitting in front of a screen, no matter how big or small that screen may be, and hating what you're viewing is not a definition of a life well lived.

The Anatomy of the Accusation
18/Dec/2020 09:32 AM

Ever since we entered into the era of the #metoo movement there has been a lot of people coming forward speaking of abuse they suffered at the hands of someone else. Add to this the #blm movement and the actions of police officers and other public officials have come under harsh scrutiny.

All bad things done to anyone is BAD. People should not say or do bad/hurtful things to anyone!

I have occasionally written about these situations in this blog over the past couple of years. I have also pointed out how some of the #metoo and #blm accusers have, themselves, been proven to be portrayers of bad deeds. But, in essence, that is not even the point—at least not the point in this piece.

Bring to mind some person you personally know or someone you know of who has pointed a finger at someone else for doing some bad deed. Look at someone who calls out someone else as having done something bad. Now, look at who that person truly is. Have they, themselves, ever done anything to hurt anyone? Or, are they perfectly pure—pure as the driven snow?

The thing is, pointing a finger, judging, or criticizing is a relatively easy thing to do. It takes very little effort. Look around you; it happens all of the time.

One of things I have noticed about a person who does a very complete presentation about the bad deeds done by someone else is that they are very rarely a pure specimens of goodness. They too have done bad deeds to others. Yet, they never mention this as a preface to judging or saying something bad about someone else. From my own personal experience(s), I look to some of the people that have done large call-outs about what someone has done to them and/or to others and I can tell you with certainty that they too have done things that have directly hurt someone else; in some cases, these people have hurt me. So, the question becomes, *"If you have hurt others do you possess a righteous standing to call out the bad deeds that have been done to you?"*

Now, each individual will have there own answer to this question. What is your? And, do you ever pose this question to yourself before you say something negative about or call-out the bad deeds of someone else?

No one is one-hundred percent pure. No one is without sin. Certainly, I am not. But, I do not spend my time creating presentations, or adding to the discussion about the wrongness of someone else.

The world is dominated by the internet; especially in terms of leisure time. So many people, with little else to do, spend their time focusing on, criticizing, and villainizing the actions of others. Yes, some people have done some very obviously bad things. But, more often than not, the people who others focus upon have done nothing more than live life from their own perspective and life-understanding. Yet, they are the ones people discuss, critique, criticize, and ultimately hurt. They do this when what that person has done has no direct affect on the life of those who are attacking them. Thus, what is the point? What does it prove? Ultimately, all it does is to damage the life of the person being focused upon thus creating negative karma for the person who instigates or takes part in the attack.

Your life is defined by what you do. Your life is defined by what you choose to do. Your life is defined by what you do to others. Most people, however, are so locked into a space of Self-ish-ness that they never even consider how their words or actions may damage the life of someone else. Thus, this is the birthplace for bad deeds being done to others. And, no matter how much one person wants to call-out what they think about or what someone else has or has not done to someone else, unless they are true to their own heart and can be honest to themselves and to others about the life-damage they have unleashed onto someone/anyone else, they should be silent as they too are not perfect—they too have hurt the life of someone else—they too have sinned.

Again, ponder the question, *"If you have hurt others do you possess a righteous standing to call out the bad deeds that have been done to you?"*

Particularly in the 1970, the books written by Carlos Castaneda were a highly influential element to modern spirituality. They depicted the author's interaction with a Mexican Indian shaman known as Don Juan. In fact, Carlos Castaneda competed his Ph.D. from U.C.L.A. by presenting his dissertation on his interactions with Don Juan which would later be published and sell millions of copies; *Don Juan: A Yaqui Way of Knowledge.* The only problem was, it was all a lie. Virtually everything presented in the dissertation/book was fiction. Yet, the man became a cultural icon and earned his Ph.D. by presenting false facts.

Me too... Back then before the truth was revealed, I too read, believed, and learned from his books.

What I am saying here is one-hundred percent easily verifiable. In fact, there have been entire books written on the subject. So, there is no new wisdom being imparted here. From this, however, the question must be asked, *"What is true knowledge?" "What is fact and what is fiction?"*

Let's step beyond the element that what he had written was not based in fact. Let's forget about that for moment... Was what he wrote educational—particularly from a spiritual perspective? Yes, it was. Obviously, it was. He sold millions of copies of his books. But, would people have purchased those books had they believed it was not the true story of his spiritual unfolding? That's hard to say. We will never know. But, as it was presented as fact, people really believed what he, or more precisely Don Juan, was teaching.

Throughout time, there have been a lot of people who have presented false illustrations of their spiritual awakening to the world. Having walked this path for most of my life, I have encountered more than few false profits and fake teachers. But, for them, it was all about ego; it was all about undiagnosed psychological inadequacy, it was all about money. They were seeking fame and fortune. Castaneda was not that way, however. In fact, he was all but a recluse. Sure, he made his money via his writings, but he was not out there on the lecture circuit where the fame and the admiration really come into play.

The question must be asked for anyone who seeks spiritual awaking and seeks it via listening to or following some other person, *"Is what they are saying true?"* And, *"If it is not, does that change their message and does it alter the fact of whether they should or should not be listened to?"*

Castaneda, in part, earned his Ph.D. via a deception about himself and his learning experience. But, U.C.L.A. never disavowed that degree. Most people who read Castaneda probably still do not know his truth. Thus, in their mind, all they read was real. They learned from it. His writings guided them. They had no reason to doubt their or his validity.

So, is a lie ever the truth? And, does it really matter if you believe it?

Can a teacher who lies be trusted? Or, does them being a liar cause their message to go mute?

You should think about these things before you ever believe anyone or anything they say because what they say, though it may even be university approved, may be a complete lie. What does that make them? What does that make what they teach? And, what does that make you for listening to and believing them in the first place?

Zen Filmmaking
and All the Crazy Things That People Say
16/Dec/2020 01:10 PM

Back in February of this year I had the idea to put together a book titled, *Zen Filmmaking and All the Crazy Things That People Say,* focusing on the reviews that have been written about my Zen Films. I got distracted and went onto other projects. Maybe I will finish it up next year. In the mean time, here's the intro I wrote for the book. You may enjoy it.

Introduction

Here's a fun book for all you fans (or haters) of *Zen Filmmaking.* Collected within these pages are many of the reviews of Zen Films that were posted on the internet over the years. Some are very positive, understanding, and praise the Zen Films while other (most) torpedo them proclaiming how horrible every aspect of every film actually is. In either case, combined, they present a fun, explicit look into the Zen craziness that is *Zen Filmmaking.* Read on and have fun.

*   *   *

Over the years since I entered the film game it has forever perplexed me how film reviewers, (professional and amateur), would take all the time and expend all of the energy necessary to write a review about an independent film they loved or hated. Of course, the reviews written by a hater of a film are always the most palpable but sometime people really love a film and write a strikingly positive review, as well. Personally, I always wondered why a reviewer would write a review instead of being imaginative in their own right and creating their own works of film art. But, that's just me.

I have always found it very disingenuous for a person who had not actually gone through the process of creating a film to become a film reviewer. Like I have long said, *"What is a film critic? With very few exceptions it is a person who doesn't have the talent or the dedication to actually create a film."* ...For if a person has not actually created a film they have no idea about the process involved and what it takes to actually envision, instigate, get the equipment, the cast and the crew together, film and then edit, soundtrack, M&E the feature, and then realize a final production. If they have never had this experience, how can they truly understand filmmaking and how can they provide a valid commentary about a film without personally understanding what it took to bring that film together? Moreover, if they were not on the specific set of the film they are discussing they have no firsthand knowledge about what actually took place or what was the motivations of the filmmaker or the experiences of the cast or the crew.

Since my early emersion in the film industry I have felt the same way as many a filmmaker has, *"It's easy to discuss what someone else has done. Let's see what you can do."* Alas, most film critics never walk down the path of creative filmmaking, however, as it is so much easier to simply sit and type on their computer's keyboard or get in front of their iMac or iPhone and discuss the productions of someone else.

Over the years I have watched as many a reviewer spoke about my Zen Films and myself. Many have actually attempted to tell their readers or listeners what I was feeling when I was creating a specific film. But, how can anyone know what another individual is feeling or why they do what they do? In virtually every case that a reviewer has spoken about my filmmaking motivations and the reasoning behind my end results, they were wrong. Wrong, but as a film critic in this day and age of self-publishing and internet forums, they encountered no checks and balances, so they could say whatever they want with no repercussions.

Some critics have even discussed how I felt about a specific review. I always found those statements immensely amusing. They never spoke to me—they never asked me how I felt... In fact, to this day, over all these many-many years and all of the films I have created, there has not been one film critic who actually spoke to me before they reviewed one of my movies. So, how could any of them have any idea about what I was feeling or why? The fact is, though a number of reviewers have discussed how I felt about a specific review, they were, in fact, wrong.

Do negative reviews bother me? I do not like negativity on any level for all it breeds is further negativity, nor do I appreciate reviewers who distort or twist the truth to their own ends in their reviews. This being said, if a review is well written, be it positive or negative, for the most part, I find them entertaining.

The thing I do not like, and I have spoken about this a lot over the years, is when a reviewer presents their opinion as fact but their opinion is, in fact, incorrect. What happens from this is that it provides a certain type of individual, who does not possess an investigative mind and does not scrutinize the supposed facts for themselves, to be exposed to falsehoods by believing the fabrications presented by the critic. This style of pseudo journalism gives birth to all kinds of misinformation and false facts being disseminated to the masses. Lies and falsehoods, based upon erroneous opinions, are a never a good thing.

I have long been an outspoken proponent of Intellectual Property Rights enforced by Copyright Law. In this digital age, most people don't care about the rights of the creator, however, as they just want to watch movies for free on unauthorized websites and grab footage from films and do whatever they want with it. Like I always say, if they were the creator of that film, they would possess a very different frame of mind, but as they are not, they do not care about the consequences this style of behavior has on the filmmaker. In fact, some on-line reviewers have become very wealthy grabbing footage from films without authorization and using that footage to create presentations. Illegal, yes. But, prosecution is very expensive, so many get away with it.

As the FBI has proclaimed, *"Internet Piracy is not a Victimless Crime."* The independent filmmaker is the one who is hurt. But, how many reviewers care as long as they are developing a following and making money off of discussing the creations of other people. And, how many viewers actually care as long as they are getting away with watching movies for free and/or being entertained by being allowed to watch or read provocative presentations based upon someone's opinion about someone else's creation?

Ever since I first created *Zen Filmmaking* it has always been about the lack of defined content. It is about freedom. It is about taking the viewer on a Mind Ride. It was never about story, story structure, or filming or acting in the traditional sense of the subject.

Since its inception, I have been very specific about what *Zen Filmmaking* was and what it was not. Yet, no matter how much information is out there about this cinematic art form, reviewers continue to get it wrong. They continue to attempt to define Zen Films within their own mental framework. They continue to attempt to put their own definition upon it and draw their own conclusion about it, comparing it to what it is not; traditional filmmaking.

Here lies the ultimate fault in the reviewer; they are attempting to put their own definition onto something that they can never truly understand. As they did not create it, they can never understand it. Thus, all they have to say about any film is solely based upon their own predetermined judgment about that film.

But remember, as it is proclaimed in Matthew 7:1-5, *"Judge not, that you be not judged. For with the judgment you pronounce you will be judged, and with the measure you use it will be measured to you. Why do you see the speck that is in your brother's eye, but do not notice the log that is in your own eye? Or how can you say to your brother, 'Let me take the speck out of your eye,' when there is the log in your own eye? You hypocrite, first take the log out of your own eye, and then you will see clearly to take the speck out of your brother's eye."*

With all this as a basis, what I am presenting in this book are reviews about my films and my filmmaking taken from the Public Domain of the World Wide Web. As everybody seems to not care about the Copyright Infractions they have done to my films and my other creative works presented in their reviews, I will hereby return the favor.

What I am doing in this book is presenting you, the reader, with the reviews and the discourses, created by film critics that have been found and referred to me by friends, foes, and fans. They are presented in their entirety with no editing in any manner.

If any of you reviewers out there have a problem with this book, think about his, I am casting your reviews to the annals of history this one and only time. There will not be a second edition of this book. Plus, perhaps this will give you the opportunity to consider the affect your reviews have had on other filmmakers and myself. With that thought in mind, from this book, maybe all of us will become more conscious and invoke a more caring process of human interaction, realizing that everything everyone does has a wide spanning effect and the artist and the creative person can never truly be judged by anyone but themselves. Like I always say, *"Think about the other person first before you do anything that may affect anyone."* Mostly, hopefully you, the reader, can have some fun reading these reviews. But remember, don't take them too seriously.

As my motto always has been, *"Be Positive,"* have fun with these reviews and see them for they are: the positive, the negative, the truthful, the distorted, and the lies. And remember, if you weren't there, you weren't there. Not being there means you have absolutely no firsthand knowledge about anything that took place.

Remember, what is the number one rule of *Zen Filmmaking?* *"Having fun is what it is all about."*

Read on and have fun!

Scott Shaw

*　　*　　*

15/Dec/2020 01:57 PM

How much of your Life Time do you spend presenting an image to the outside world so that other people will consider you a Something?

*   *   *

15/Dec/2020 08:23 AM

Right now you could do something that would
someone else's life better.

THE
ZEN